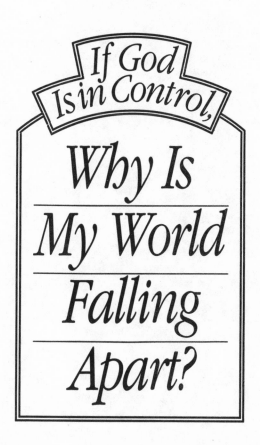

If God
Is in Control,

Why Is
My World
Falling
Apart?

Verna Birkey

If God Is in Control,

Why Is My World Falling Apart?

MULTNOMAH

Portland, Oregon 97266

Unless otherwise indicated, Scripture references are from the New King James Bible, copyright Thomas Nelson, Inc. 1979, 1980, 1982, 1988.

Scripture references marked NIV are from the Holy Bible: New International Version, copyright 1973, 1978, 1984 by the International Bible Society. Used by permission of Zondervan Bible Publishers.

Scripture references marked TLB are from The Living Bible, copyright 1971 by Tyndale House Publishers, Wheaton, Ill. Used by permission.

Scripture references marked Phillips are from J.B. Phillips: The New Testament in Modern English. Copyright J.B. Phillips 1958, 1960, 1972 by Macmillan Publishing Co., Inc.

Scripture references marked NASB are from the New American Standard Bible, copyright the Lockman Foundation 1960, 1962, 1963, 1968, 1971, 1973, 1975, 1977.

Scripture references marked AMP are from The Amplified Bible, copyright 1969 Zondervan Publishing House.

Scripture references marked KJV are from the King James Version.

Cover design by Bruce DeRoos

For more information on the Enriched Living Workshops taught by Verna Birkey write: P.O. Box 3039, Kent, WA 98032

IF GOD IS IN CONTROL, WHY IS MY WORLD FALLING APART?
© 1990 by Verna Birkey
Published by Multnomah Press
Portland, Oregon 97266

Multnomah Press is a ministry of Multnomah School of the Bible,
8435 N.E. Glisan Street, Portland, Oregon 97220

Printed in the United States of America

Library of Congress Cataloging-in-Publication Data

Birkey, Verna
    If God is in control, why is my world falling apart? / Verna Birkey.
      p.   cm.
    Includes bibliographical references.
    ISBN 0-88070-393-8
    1. Providence and government of God. 2. Christian life—1960-
I. Title.
BT96.2.B57   1990
231'.5—dc20   90-41717
                                                      CIP

90 91 92 93 94 - 5 4 3 2 1

Contents

A Word Before   7

Part 1
Who in the World Is in Charge?

1. He's Got the Whole World in His Hands   13
2. Father Knows Best   19
3. Father's Incredible Promise   31
4. Is Everything Under God's Control?   39
5. The Bigger Picture: God's Master Plan   55

Part 2
Who in My World Can I Trust?

6. Restfully Sure of God's Loving Control   71
7. Does This End All Our Struggles?   87
8. Why Do I Find It Hard to Trust God?   99
9. Does God Really Care About Me?   111

Part 3
How in the World Should I Live?

10. Unoffended with the Unexplained   123
11. Am I Just a Passive Puppet?   135
12. Attitude: Gratitude   149
13. The Bottom Line   163

Notes   175

God is the Blessed Controller of all,
And I can trust Him whatever befall;
All things will work together for good,
This is His promise to me in His Word.

Blessed Controller of all things,
Safe in His care my rejoicing heart sings;
His mighty power is working for me,
Trusting His love my spirit is free.

Oh, how I praise Him! Oh, how I sing!
Blessed Controller of everything;
Trusting His goodness, wisdom, and power,
Knowing He loves me through every hour.

Verna Birkey
Copyright 1977

(May be sung to the tune "Blessed Assurance.")

A Word Before

This book had its roots in the very beginnings of my Christian walk. I can't really tell you just how it happened, but gradually I walked into the understanding that God—my loving Father—is behind all the encounters, events, and circumstances of my life.

The next step was when J. B. Phillips shared with the world his clear, fresh paraphrase of the New Testament. His translation of 1 Timothy 6:15 has had a profound effect on my personal life, and it has rippled on out to others. To know and rest in the truth that, indeed, "God is the Blessed Controller of all things" has been of incomparable worth in my life.

I have talked about this concept with thousands of women and men and young people over the past decades and have received more mail on this than on any other segment of teaching. People want something to hold on to. Some solid ground when life seems to be shaking and their world caving in. We find that solid ground here.

Although theologically honest, this is not a book of theology. It is a book for the heart.

Because I want you to take what you read through your mind, into your heart, and out into your daily responses, I highly recommend you follow each chapter by working through the questions in *Making It Personal*. These questions given at the end of the chapters may be done in individual or group study.

Writing a book is not a one-person project. My thanks . . .

To Jeanette Turnquist, my long-time friend and teammate in ministry. I couldn't have done it without you, Nettie. I'm thankful for the skills God has given you, and for your perseverance. You have labored diligently and cheerfully—researching, organizing, refining, tirelessly rewriting section by section, adding warmth and clarity. And hats off to you also for the practical Bible study material in *Making It Personal*.

To the women who have attended the Enriched Living Seminars, for sharing your struggles, your victories, and for letting me know the peace you are experiencing through walking in the truth of 1 Timothy 6:15.

To my old "friends" who have given me fuel to

understand and relate this truth to my own life—F. B. Meyer, Oswald Chambers, Amy Carmichael, Hannah Whitall Smith. You'll meet them all as you read, and I recommend you make them your friends too.

To Liz Heaney, my editor-friend at Multnomah, for reigning Nettie and me in and deftly guiding us in our final stages of writing.

Who in the World
Is in Charge?

Divine Kingship. *When we grasp that idea, it becomes the dominant note of life. It is the master-key which opens every lock. Just to believe, deep down in your soul, that the Father of Jesus—our Father—is King. That the God who is moved by the fall of a little bird from its nest, is King of the world and all its forces, and of everything in human life. To know and believe this is to get something which is worth everything else.*

F. B. Meyer, *Our Daily Walk*

CHAPTER ONE

He's Got the Whole World in His Hands

Cornfields and cattle barns sped by on both sides. The cows would soon need to be milked, and the harvest would soon be ripe. But these reminders of the orderly flow of God's ways seemed out of place to Tim and Shelley as they followed the ambulance down the familiar country road. Today their world did not appear to be following in that same safe, orderly path.

No, if things had been as usual, little Zach would be strapped in the seat beside them. Today kind paramedics hovered over him. If things had been as usual, his two older brothers would be dangling shiny toys over his bed, and his big blue eyes would be sparkling and his eager hands reaching. Today his eyes had emitted pain and fear as Tim and Shelley had watched the ambulance doors close them out.

Zach was born with a rare blood disease and had needed extra care ever since that time. None of their days with this special boy were ordinary, but this one held a new and frightening prospect. Zach had fallen, and the result was a cranial bleed. Shelley wrote:

"When we got to the hospital and on through the night, he seemed to do great. The next morning when Tim and I walked into the intensive care unit, Zachie was very fussy. I started to give him a bottle, but something seemed different. He was looking at me, but it didn't seem as though he could see me. Then he began having seizures. His pupils remained fixed and dilated, even after the seizures stopped.

"They rushed him down for a CAT scan. As the lab door closed us out, I heard the Lord gently say, 'Shelley, what if I take him home?' Then, 'What if I let him live and remain blind?' Then, 'What if I leave him as a vegetable?'

"The questions seemed painfully familiar. Was it already a year since I had struggled to commit our precious baby into God's hands—and to take my hands off? I had faced some hard questions then too. Now I found myself saying, 'Lord, I meant it a year ago when I said that Zach is yours! If you want to let him live, I will bless you. If you allow him to be only a vegetable, I will embrace this also. If he is blind, your grace will be sufficient.'

"Then I quoted Philippians 1:19-20 which I had memorized: 'For I know that this shall turn out for my deliverance through your prayers and the provision of the Spirit of Jesus Christ, according to my earnest expectation and hope, that I shall not be put to shame in anything, but that with all boldness, Christ shall even now, as always, be exalted in my body, whether by life or by death' (NASB).

"As we waited, God's ruling peace remained constant and His tender hand seemed quietly resting around our shoulders, as a loving earthly father's would be. Soon the specialist came out and told us that the hemorrhaging had decreased and what we were seeing was a post-trauma manifestation that should clear in a day or so.

"Zach is doing beautifully today. Such a contrast to three days ago. From blind eyes, with shadows of death lurking behind, to eyes sparkling with the very essence of life!

"Our family now understands a new level of reality in the truth of Psalm 23. We truly 'feared no evil,' for God was with us. All of us experienced this as we each—individually and together—were able to roll our cares on Him. We each knew the ruling peace of Christ.

"But, Verna, I want you to know that the two significant, sustaining, and comforting truths that produced such supernatural peace are: God is good and God is sovereign. Our blessed Lord, who is in control, saw us through those critical days. We are purposing to walk by faith in the light of these comforting truths. Our God is good! Our God reigns!"

Comfort through Thick Static

As I read Shelley's letter, I recalled how this truth first became real to me. In our comfortable old farm house in central Illinois, Mother faithfully listened to our one distant Christian radio station from Chicago. Much of the time the words filtered through thick static, but Mother persistently listened to the messages and songs until all was static and nothing could be understood. Sometimes it seemed she was comforted by the static, knowing there was some message of God's goodness and love behind it all.

Despite the interference, one program and its theme song made a strong impression on my teenage mind.

God is still on the throne,
And He will remember His own;
Though trials may press us
And burdens distress us,
He never will leave us alone.

God is still on the throne,
He never forsaketh His own;
His promise is true,
He will not forget you,
God is still on the throne.[1]

Truly, "Our God is in heaven; He does whatever He pleases" (Psalm 115:3). "The LORD has established His throne in heaven, and His kingdom rules over all" (Psalm 103:19). He is still on the throne!

In this time of staggering changes in our world, it is good to affirm that our loving Lord reigns in the earth and in the affairs of men. But it is most comforting to know and believe that God rules in the daily circumstances of my personal life. Nothing in His world is out of His control. As Bev Shea sings with such confidence, "He's got the whole wide world in His hands. And He has you and me in His hands. He's got the whole world in His hands."

Yes, life *is* different when I affirm God is ruling in my current circumstances. As I write today, an unusual world of white has enclosed my little house. We were warned that this snowy deep-freeze from Alaska would descend overnight and drastically change our normally balmy Seattle weather.

I live in a land of hills and valleys, in a land where snow removal equipment is scarce because it is seldom needed. The streets have quickly become like ice skating rinks, and most of us transplanted mid-westerners have lost the marvelous art of winter driving.

Tomorrow morning at six I'm scheduled on Flight 1069 bound for Boise where I'm committed to speak all day on Saturday. The questions come: Will the roads be passable by then? What if I can't get to the plane? Will I have to cancel? How will I let three hundred ladies know?

Questions? Yes, but God Still Reigns

My questions help me to realistically plan the best ways to achieve my goal—keeping my commitment to speak in Boise tomorrow. But underlying all the questions is a deep-settled assurance that, yes, despite these circumstances, God is still on the throne. The storm with its uncertainties and inconveniences has not taken Him by surprise—even if the weather makes it impossible to get to Boise!

How could Tim and Shelley declare "God is good; God is sovereign," even as they faced the unavoidable uncertainties of the future with little Zach? What can bring us to a place of trust during large or small crises, those times when we feel our world is falling apart?

Those questions are what this book is all about.

Happiness, Heaven itself, is nothing else but a perfect conformity, a cheerful and eternal compliance of all the powers of the soul with the Will of God.

Samuel Shaw,
Joy and Strength

CHAPTER TWO

Father Knows Best

Today was Jon Kent Witmer's day! A dream come true. Jon Kent, a young, creative, inventive, adventuresome risk-taker, had been working patiently for months designing and building his own gyrocopter.

His proud but somewhat awestruck parents stood together at the local airport. He had definitely wanted them to be there, and they wanted to show their support of his accomplishment. They felt the usual apprehension any parent would have as their son ascended into the sky in his homemade aircraft. But with three sons and a daughter, they were getting used to letting their children "spread their wings" and try new things. Today it was no longer a figure of speech. Yes, they would be with Jon Kent today as they had been in each new achievement through the years—celebrating and joining in his joy.

Their hands shaded the sun from their eyes as they followed his movement up and then as he circled over the airport. But the copter's graceful progress suddenly jackknifed as a major malfunction occurred and the aircraft somersaulted to the ground. It was an unbelievable moment. The parents stood transfixed for a fraction of a second. On the ground, a few hundred feet away, were the crumpled remains of the gyrocopter, but no movement of life. No more excited anticipation. No more cheers. In their place only an abrupt and paralyzing fear.

What could bring this mom and dad through the dark tunnel of watching their son plunge to his death?

Another parent in pain wrote, "In April our eighteen-year-old daughter was killed by a drunken driver. Our hearts were broken, confused, and so very, very hurt."

What could bring this mother to experience peace during tremendous grief and pain?

"I was an excessive worrier," another wrote. "My husband used to say the first thing I did in the morning was to decide what I had to worry about that day. During the past year our family experienced enough trauma to give me fuel for worry for years to come. In April I took a bad fall down the basement steps. In May I had recovered to the point of walking without pain when our grass caught on fire. In putting it out I stepped on a nail and got blood poisoning.

"About that time my husband was injured mowing

the lawn and was rushed to the hospital. The next week, after we had recovered from these events, I was kicked by a horse and spent six weeks on crutches. Two weeks later our daughter was severely injured by a pony and eventually had four operations to correct the problems. Our son developed lumps under his arms which the doctors indicated may be leukemia. *It was during those three months that the Lord taught me not to worry.*"

What could possibly turn a chronic worrier into a non-worrier, even through three months of calamity after calamity?

Coupled with a deep assurance that He actually cares for *me*, the truth of God's loving control is one of the most peace-producing concepts in all of Scripture. But what can bring one to that place of trust? Let me take you on the journey that has led some of us there.

The Circle of God's Will

Let this circle represent the sphere of God's will: God's way for us . . . His plan for our lives. And we will also include in this what He *allows* to happen to us in

life—His permissive will. The X inside the circle represents the person whose basic life-thrust is to go God's way. He or she is committed to Jesus Christ as Savior, owns Him as Lord and Master, and wants to follow in His way.[1]

If our deepest desire is to *follow the way of God*, to live in agreement with Him and have His will fulfilled in us, then that X represents you and it represents me. We have responded to God's call to us through Paul when he said:

"I beseech you therefore, brethren, by the mercies of God, that you present your bodies a living sacrifice, holy, acceptable to God, which is your reasonable service. And do not be conformed to this world, but be transformed by the renewing of your mind, that you may prove what is that good and acceptable and perfect will of God" (Romans 12:1, 2).

Keep Off the Detours

A sign on the desk of George Sweeting, a former President of Moody Bible Institute, read, "Keep off the detours." A subtle but poignant reminder that till the end of his life, his single-minded purpose was a solid commitment to walk in the ways of God and the specific plan God had for him. It's a decision, a choice to be made today and affirmed every succeeding day in every circumstance of life, till Jesus comes.

That desire to walk in God's way is the same attitude Jesus had and expressed in so many ways:

"My food is to do the will of Him who sent Me, and to finish His work" (John 4:34).

"For I have come down from Heaven, not to do what I want, but to do the will of him who sent me" (John 6:38, Phillips).

"I always do those things that please Him" (John 8:29).

Jesus single-mindedly walked in God's ways as He revealed them step by step. The supreme expression of this commitment came during those closing days of His life and the trying hours in the Garden as He poured out His heart to the Father to "remove this cup" from Him. But when the cup remained, His sincere and unqualified prayer continued to be, "Not My will, but Yours, be done" (Luke 22:42).

Committed to God's Will

For us, the first mile of the journey toward the peace that Jon Kent Witmer's parents knew is this same commitment to the will of God which Jesus had. It is not, "*My* will, not yours, be done." Rather, like Jesus, we must be committed to choosing God's will above our own will, above our own preferences, above our own desires.

God's ultimate and general will for His children is that we become more and more Christ-like, that we increasingly become "conformed to the image of His Son" (Romans 8:29). In addition, He promises to lead each of us in the way we (individually) should go. As we delight in His will, we can be sure He will direct us in our specific path. He shows this path to us through Scripture, and He may use the voice of circumstances, or the advice of a trusted, godly friend to confirm His direction. Or He may use all of these. One thing is sure: God never guides us into sin, nor does He ever expect us to do anything contrary to His Word.[2]

It is reassuring to know that He wills what is best for us, that His will, which we are embracing, is "good, acceptable, and perfect." Many of God's children have a wrong view of His will. They think it's difficult, harsh, or against their best interests. Some even think God is out to make them miserable and take away all those things, people, or even ministries in which they find joy. But our loving heavenly Father is not like that.

" 'For I know the plans that I have for you,' declares the LORD, 'plans for welfare and not for calamity to give you a future and a hope' " (Jeremiah 29:11, NASB).

As He assures us in this verse, He is interested in our personal welfare, our best interests. The love God has for us is wrapped up in His goodness, and He is bent on doing what is best for us. Numerous times in the book of Deuteronomy, the refrain comes, "that it may be well with you."[3] This was God's heart for His people then, and no less for us today.

"For years," Carolyn reported, "to me 'doing God's will' meant doing something difficult, something I didn't want to do. From the time I was twelve I worked in church in some aspect, but I could not really say I derived joy from it. It was just something that I was supposed to do as a Christian. In fact, I think if I had gotten joy from it, I would have felt I was not 'doing God's will' because it would have seemed very selfish to me. It's as though I thought God always gives spinach and never anything tasty like chocolate cake."

"I am afraid there are some, even of God's own children," Hannah Smith writes, "who scarcely think that He is equal to themselves in tenderness, and love, and thoughtful care; and who, in their secret thoughts, charge Him with a neglect and indifference of which they would feel themselves incapable. The truth really is that His care is infinitely superior to any possibilities of human care; and that He, who counts the very hairs of our heads, and suffers not a sparrow to fall without Him, takes note of the minutest matters that can affect the lives of His children, and regulates them all according to His own perfect will, let their origin be what they may.

"He is our Father, and He loves us, and He knows just what is best, and therefore, of course, His will is the very most blessed thing that can come to us under any circumstances. . . . But it really would seem as if God's own children were more afraid of His will than of anything else in life, His lovely, lovable will, which only means loving-kindnesses and tender mercies, and blessings unspeakable to their souls!"[4]

When I agree that the will of God for me is good, and when I know He has my best interests in view, I can say, "Yes, Lord, Your will be done."

Amy Carmichael puts it in her usual penetrating way, "There are two prayers, one of which we are constantly praying, sometimes in words, sometimes in thoughts, always in actions. One is, 'Teach me to do the thing that pleaseth *Thee*'; the other is, 'Lord, let me do the thing that pleaseth *me*.' If we are honest with our God He will show us which of these two prayers we habitually use. Some use the first in the morning, and the second all through the day; for such, the second is the habit of the soul. Some vary between the two, and that leads to an up-and-down life. Some are growing more and more into the first as an all-day prayer, and their lives are growing stronger and gladder, more equable, more dependable, and much more peaceful."[5]

Am I Living within the Circle?

We need to ask ourselves: Am I living within the circle of God's will for me? Here I'm referring to a deeper relationship than merely claiming that Christ is my Savior and then going my own way. Rather, am I committed to going His way, to walking in obedience to His will—not wanting to go counter to His will, but to cooperate with Him? Have I made that basic life choice to seek His will and way above my own?

Christie grew up in a family with four talented sisters. Gradually, she became aware that each of her sisters was able to sing well and even play an instrument, but she couldn't do either. Painfully shy because of her buck teeth, she wondered if she had any talents. Certainly, she concluded, she could never be a speaker, a song leader, a cheerleader, a teacher, or anything that required her to be in front of others. That she just couldn't bear!

"Before reaching my teens, I was intensely aware of what an untalented, unattractive, 'ugly duckling' I was," Christie wrote. "If I could just crawl into a hole and disappear, I knew no one would miss me, but at 5'6" there was no hole large enough!"

To make matters even worse, a smack on her head in an accident resulted in seizures and a terrible loss of memory. The seizures kept her constantly depressed and forced her to drop driver's education, the new love of this fifteen-year-old!

High school was a very lonely time with no true friends, but during that time her deep friendship with the Lord began to develop and she began to believe in God's goodness. She reasoned, "Surely, if God made me as I am, He must see something in me He could use. Perhaps it would be marriage. But hearing Grandmother's sad story, I determined to wait for God's choice for me and to keep myself pure for 'him.' My younger sister seemed determined to prove that my idea of 'keeping myself pure' was old-fashioned. According to her, I would end up an 'old maid,' while she had all the fun. And fun she had! Deep down I knew she was wrong."

At college, Christie was amazed that some young men seemed interested in her. One fellow was asking for dates on a regular basis. This was beyond her greatest dreams. Why did he like her? Although braces had remedied her crooked teeth, she still suffered from a poor memory, unstable emotions, and depression.

"Then one weekend it happened," she went on telling her story. "My 'Prince Charming' turned from me and dated an upperclassman twice. My world seemed to be caving in! I had been so sure that the Lord was leading us together. Blinded by tears, I found my way to a little room and poured out my heart to God. I don't know how long I spent on my knees, for a battle was raging in my heart, but finally His love won and I submitted to Him. 'Lord,' I prayed, 'if it is your will for me to have this awful memory, to take medicine for the rest of my life to stabilize my emotions, to never drive, and even to never marry, I want your will more than I want any of these.'

"I can't explain the flood of peace that came over me as I gave the Lord my most treasured dream for marriage and my expectations for physical and emotional normalcy. When my tears were dry and I could smile again, my eyes caught sight of a plaque on the wall of that little prayer room, *Not in endeavor, not in aloofness, not in forgetting, but in acceptance lies peace.*

"That was the secret. As I truly accepted God's will for me, He gave me His peace. What I didn't realize at the time was that as I made this commitment to accept what He allowed in my life, He was free to begin healing and causing my memory to improve. The seizures became fewer and finally disappeared. I was able to get my driver's license. And to my amazement and thrill, God allowed me to marry my Prince Charming!"

In her own eyes, Christie's assets were meager or nil. No beauty, no talents, not even emotional health. But it was these very "debits" that brought her to the point of accepting God's will for her life. Her last comment to me was, "My sister is still, to this day, paying dearly for the few years of 'fun' she had in going her own way."

Yielding to God's will does not assure us that our circumstances will improve, but it is the first step to heart rest in the face of a heartache. The alternative is to be bent on having my selfish way and to reap the fruit of bitterness and unrest. Sometimes there is a subtle, sweet, quiet, stubborn, inward resistance, and a clinging to my own way which I am not willing to recognize. It is good to ask the Holy Spirit for His gentle work of instruction and illumination.

If my heart's cry is to embrace the will of God, if my prayer is, "Teach me to do the thing that pleases You," then I am living inside the circle of His will and can claim His promises.

Making It Personal

1. What negative ideas have you or some of your friends had about the will of God?

2. Express in your own words what it means to live inside the circle of God's will.

3. How did each of the following people express his or her commitment to God's will and ways? What can you learn from these that will deepen your own commitment?

Noah: Genesis 6:9-22, Hebrews 11:7

Abraham: Genesis 12:1, 4; 22:1-19; Hebrews 11:8, 17-19

Moses: Hebrews 11:24-26

Eli: 1 Samuel 3:10-18

David: Psalm 25:4, 5; 40:8; 119:14-16; 143:8-10

Solomon: Psalm 72:18, 19; Proverbs 3:5, 6

Mary: Luke 1:38

Jesus: Matthew 26:39; John 4:34, 5:30

Paul: Acts 20:24; 21:13, 14; 2 Corinthians 12:7-10; Philippians 3:7-14

4. What is God's ultimate purpose (goal, will) for each of His children? See Romans 8:29; Colossians 1:28; 2 Corinthians 3:18, 4:11.

5. What are some other clear areas of God's will for His children?

Matthew 18:14
John 6:39, 40

Ephesians 5:17-22, 25, 33; 6:1-9
Colossians 1:9-12
1 Thessalonians 4:3-7, 5:18
1 Timothy 2:1, 2
1 Peter 2:13-17

6. How do I know that God wills what is best for me? (Refer to page 23.)

7. What are some of the benefits that are ours when we line up our will with God's will?

Psalm 119:1, 2
John 7:17, 13:17, 15:10
Ephesians 6:2, 3
1 John 3:22

8. Each morning this week, ask the Lord to help you check out which prayer you are consciously or unconsciously praying during the day:

Let me do what pleases me, or
Teach me to do what pleases You.

At the end of the day, think through your attitudes and actions, again praying the Lord will reveal your habit of life in this respect.

9. Write out your own commitment to the will of God. Include a general statement which can be renewed daily, and some specific areas that currently relate to your life. Reading through this chapter again may give you some ideas.

I will charge my soul to believe and wait for Him, and will follow His providence, and not go before it, nor stay behind it.

Samuel Rutherford,
Joy and Strength

CHAPTER THREE

Father's Incredible Promise

For twenty years, Dr. Helen Roseveare served as a medical missionary in Zaire. During the 1964 Simba rebellion, she watched with sorrow as several of her co-workers were cruelly beaten and brutally murdered. She herself was stomped on by the guerrilla soldiers till her nose, jaw, and several ribs were broken. Constantly moved from one prison camp to another, she never knew what would happen next. Rape was common.

"I had, in advance," Helen wrote, "geared myself to accept that God had the right to require anything of me that fit into His purpose. God was the Lord of my life and I trusted Him completely. [During that time] I learned that God is always present-tense. . . . When He says, 'My grace is sufficient,' He means it. It's not, 'My grace will be sufficient for tomorrow's problems. . . . It is, 'My grace is sufficient for your immediate, present-tense needs.' "[1]

Helen Roseveare was fully committed to the will of God and knew what it meant to claim the promise of 2 Corinthians 12:9 in her present situation. If we are people committed to going God's way, living inside the circle of His will, we too have the privilege of claiming the promises He has given His children in His Word.

GOD'S WILL
Claim Promises
Romans 8:28
X

That is, I can take a promise such as Romans 8:28, claim it (declare it as a fact), and confidently trust that God will make it true in my present set of circumstances: "And we know that all things work together for good to those who love God, to those who are the called according to His purpose."

Reading this carefully, I realize God is actually telling me He is making this incredible promise true in the particular events of my life today and every day. That is, God is superintending all the activities, people, and situations that will touch my life. He will see to it that all these conditions will work together for good. For whose good—God's or ours? Both. Because of what we know of God's goodness and love to us (see Chapter 9), we can be sure it will work for our good. And because we know that God will not give His glory to another, we can be sure it will also work for His good and for His glory.

That's My Problem

Notice, however, the promise is conditional. It's not made to everyone, but to "those who love God, to those who are the called according to His purpose." No doubt someone is thinking, *That's my problem. I don't know if I love the Lord enough to qualify.*

It's not how much love I *feel* toward God that qualifies me for claiming this promise. Emotions are not the measure of true love. Jesus said, "If you love me, you will obey what I command" (John 14:15, NIV). Obedience is the measure of genuine love to Him. The essence of true love is more in the *will* than in the emotions. It is essential that we do not look to our emotions, our feelings, as a gauge of our love in our spiritual life, or even in our natural life.

In dependence upon the power of the Spirit, with our will we make our choice to go God's way. Whether or not our emotions affirm that choice is not important. I am resolved—committed—to live in agreement with Him. Therefore, if I am God's child and desire to live in obedience to Him, even though my obedience may be imperfect, I qualify. I am living inside the circle of God's will and have the privilege of claiming God's promises.

However, in order to accomplish His own larger purposes and because of His mercy and grace which reaches out to everyone, God often brings blessing to His children who are not walking in His way, and even to those who are not His children.

" . . . The goodness of God leads you to repentance" (Romans 2:4).

" . . . He makes His sun rise on the evil and on the good, and sends rain on the just and on the unjust" (Matthew 5:45).

As these scriptures state, God may do good to the just and the unjust, but those who can *claim* His promises and *take the comfort* from them are those who are walking in obedience to His will, cooperating with Him, living inside the circle of His will.

If my heart's cry is, "Lord, teach me to do the thing that pleases You," then I can claim His promises. The one we are focusing on here is Romans 8:28, "All things work together for good to those who love God." Or as another version reads, "God causes all things to work together for good" (NASB).

Romans 8:28 doesn't say that all circumstances *are good*. Nor does it say that God *causes* all things to happen. (More on this in Chapter 10.) Many things may come to us from the evil motives and intentions of others, but God is big enough and His promise is good enough to see to it that, in the end, it will all work together for our good as we are yielded to Him and trusting Him.

The promised *good* will issue in the form of character-building or in fulfilling greater and larger purposes in God's economy than we can imagine at the moment. What a promise! What hope and confidence we can have in the midst of the difficulty, pain, and suffering.

None of These Circumstances Seemed Good

I was exhausted after three years of a rigorous schedule of teaching Bible in the schools in Alabama. The doctor had ordered tea and toast until my digestive track got back to normal. Without regular food, my already depleted body was getting weaker each day. As the days went by, this weakness seemed to generate in me a fearful sense of, "Am I losing my mind?"

Finally, I asked my roommate to call the doctor and see if I could have something more to eat. When he understood how literally I had taken his instructions for "tea and toast," he ordered, "Give that girl some food!"

By the time I got to my parents' home for a month of total rest, I was at the bottom both physically and emotionally. Day moved on to day. For a while they all seemed alike. Garden-fresh vegetables, country-fresh air, and time to read, to think, to listen to what God had to say to me all blended together till I even began to take an interest in a stack of letters that had come from some of the campers at our Bible camp the previous summer.

At camp we had taught the importance of a Quiet Time with the Lord each day. We had challenged the campers to set aside a daily time, but we had given them little concrete help as to how to put it into practice. Now, as I read the letters, a similar thread showed through. One after another said something like, "Miss B, please help me. I want to have a Quiet Time with the Lord each day, but I don't know how. Can you give me some suggestions?"

My days of recuperation and regaining strength suddenly were not purposeless. The campers' need pressed me into my first attempt at writing and publishing. The devotional guide I developed was used for many years to lead campers into a meaningful daily time with the Lord in His Word.

From my perspective, none of the circumstances that brought this about were good. Being physically and emotionally depleted was frightening and uncomfortable. I had to leave my work, and others had to do double duty to cover for me. I had the humiliation of having to admit my weakness. But God was working these things together for good.

For my good: I learned to turn from my self-sufficiency to a deeper dependence on the Lord. I learned to give Him my reputation. I had more time to spend with the Lord. The devotional book gave me courage to try further attempts at ministering to the needs of others through writing.

For the campers' good: They had the help they were asking for. We no longer just *told* them the importance, joys, and benefits of having a personal Quiet Time. We now could give them concrete helps in *how to do it.*

For Now, Content with the Promise

In many cases, it will be months or even years after the distressing event, the difficulty, the heartache, the rejection, that we will see the realization of God's promise.[2] I didn't see the full scope of God's purposes of that time until recently.

On a radio interview Dr. Helen Roseveare was asked, "Have you seen any good come from your horrible experience of being raped and beaten?" "Yes," she recalled. "I have seen good come in a number of ways, but one has been especially meaningful." After speaking at a college, she noticed two girls lingering near the front. "The older of the two came up to me, 'Could you please speak with my sister? Five weeks ago she was raped and has not spoken one word since.' In the space of a few brief moments, the girl threw her arms around me and broke into heart-rending sobs. For the next two hours we wept and shared together as she poured out all her feelings and hurts.

"Later that night as I went to bed, reflecting back on the dreadful experiences I went through during those dark nights deep in the Congo many years earlier, I could see how God does bring good from evil."[3]

Sometimes we may never see how God has blended life together for good until we see Him face to face. *Then* all life's mysteries will be made plain, and we will see how His love and power worked good for us in that situation which seemed disastrous. *Now* we may need to be content with the promise, not knowing the final outcome. Our Lord Jesus died with a question on His lips, "My God, My God, why have You forsaken Me?" (Matthew 27:46).

We may not understand, but we can trust in what He has promised.

But what about those who have not chosen to go God's way, those who live outside the circle of His will? How do I deal with the consequences of their choices and lifestyle which may mean hurt and pain for me?

Making It Personal

1. Who has the privilege of claiming God's promises and taking the comfort from them?

2. This incredible promise that all things will work together for good is given to:

- Those who love God (1 John 4:9, 10, 16, 19)

- Those who are the called according to His purpose (Romans 8:29, 30; 1 Corinthians 1:9; Ephesians 4:1-3; 1 Thessalonians 2:12; 1 Peter 2:9).

How do the verses above clarify this?

3. What is the ultimate proof of God's desire and ability to work good on our behalf? See Romans 8:32.

4. Read Romans 8:28 from several versions. Choose the one that makes it most clear for you, and write it on a card to carry with you. On the other side of the card, write your commitment to the will of God which you

wrote after Chapter 2. Review these before the Lord daily this week.

5. What are several misconceptions we may have about Romans 8:28?

6. What did Jesus say about the measure of our love for Him? See John 14:15, 23, 24.

How does John add to your understanding of this? See 1 John 2:3-6, 5:3.

7. What are some additional "incredible promises" given to us from our loving, caring Father God?

Psalm 23:6
Isaiah 43:25, 46:4
Ephesians 1:3, 4, 7, 8
Philippians 4:19
2 Peter 1:3, 4

8. Relate a time when Romans 8:28 met a special need in your life.

9. Can you list some of the "all things" in your life that God is currently working towards the end of good for you, for others involved, and for Himself? Include both the pleasant and the difficult.

10. Will you take these things one at a time and thank Him, not necessarily for the difficulty, but for that which He is working on your behalf whether you can see it or not?

11. Look at this list of "all things" once more. At this point can you see any good resulting?

His Father said, Before the trouble can meet thee it must pass through the brightness of My encompassing Presence, and passing through that brightness it loseth its darkness.

Amy Carmichael,
His Thoughts Said, His Father Said

CHAPTER FOUR

Is Everything Under God's Control?

Not everyone is interested in going God's way. Some are more interested in going their own way and focusing on what pleases themselves. Some act out of greed or jealousy, and we may be the victims of their actions.

By her own description, Vicki was a "bean pole," the untalented member of the family. Her sister who was gifted, beautiful, and popular often threw depreciating remarks at her. She "stole" Vicki's boyfriends and then taunted her to lower her standards and have "fun."

To Vicki's great surprise, one of the fellows at church began dating her. It was a very innocent, enjoyable relationship until her sister decided that she'd show Vicki *how it was done*. During the summer, she and the fellow Vicki had been dating worked at the same camp. When they returned home, he was *hers*, "hook, line, and sinker." "See," she bragged with contempt, "boys aren't happy with a *nice* girl."

All through their growing-up years, Vicki suffered intense emotional pain because of the selfishness and insensitivity of her sister.

The Circle of God's Control

Is God limited by the wrong choices people around us make? Can He do anything with or to that person who is not walking in His ways? Yes.

So, in our diagram we must place an X outside the circle of God's will to represent that person who isn't interested in cooperating with God. He or she does *not* desire to walk in line with His purposes. The person is *not* willing to bring his or her will into agreement with God's will. This one may try to control us, the people in his or her life—either openly or with cunning—so that we will do as he or she desires. And sometimes that brings great pain to us.

We draw a bigger circle which now includes both (1) the person who has chosen to go God's way and (2) the person who is not interested in cooperating with God's purposes and who might even make life difficult for the one who is. God is God—all-knowing, all-powerful,

all-wise. He reigns over the world of people and events. Even though a person may not embrace His *will*, no one can escape being within the sphere of His over-all *control*.[1] We will call this outer circle the circle of God's control.

The words *God's control* are used in the sense that God is bigger than any person or situation that touches our lives, not in the sense that God controls us like puppets on a string. He doesn't manipulate us. He doesn't force or coerce a person to operate in a certain way against his or her choices. No, He has given us a will and the power to choose. Therefore, sometimes we find ourselves subjects of the evil choices and actions of others or recipients of unwanted and even devastating circumstances.

Joseph's brothers are an excellent example of this. God did not put hate in their hearts for Joseph—they *chose* to hate him. However, God's purposes for Joseph (and ultimately His whole world-purpose through the situation) were far higher than the pain and sorrow Joseph experienced temporarily because of his brothers' choice to go the way of hate. And in the end Joseph, his whole family, and his whole nation were saved. In this sense, God was the overall orchestrator of events.[2]

You Meant It for Evil, but God . . .

Joseph found rest and comfort in the fact that One bigger than himself, bigger than all the people who misunderstood him, mistreated him, rejected him, lied about him, and forgot their promises to him was in control and could be trusted. In each valley experience in Joseph's life, he responded to the adversity with acceptance and trust so that others realized God was with him. As he calmly trusted, God caused him to be successful and honored by those in charge so that he was given responsibility and authority wherever he was—in prison or in the palace.

When Joseph's brothers recognized him as the one to whom they had been so cruel, Joseph didn't take vengeance by denying them grain, nor did he take this opportunity to shame them or get even with them for the evil they had done to him earlier. Rather, he spoke kindly to comfort them, recognizing God's hand in it all.

"Do not therefore be grieved or angry with yourselves because you sold me here; for God sent me before you to preserve life. . . . to preserve a posterity for you in the earth . . . So now *it was not you who sent me here, but God*; and He has made me a father to Pharaoh, and lord of all his house, and a ruler throughout all the land of Egypt." And again, "*As for you, you meant evil against me; but God meant it for good . . .*" (Genesis 45:5, 7, 8; 50:20, italics added).

Though his brothers had acted out of jealousy and hate, Joseph looked beyond the wickedness they had intentionally done to him and acknowledged God was using it to accomplish His purposes. He gave God the credit for all the good things that happened to him and trusted God in the adversities, whether they came through people with good or evil intentions.

In Ecclesiastes, Solomon refers to the ups and downs of life as times of prosperity and times of adversity—easy times and hard times, happy times and heavy times. That is what life is like. Solomon admonishes us to consider that God is in control of both. In fact, he says, "Surely God has appointed the one as well as the other" (Ecclesiastes 7:14).

There will be times in your life and mine marked

by peace and quiet, gaiety and laughter, when the road is easy and smooth. And then there will be times when life is heavy, the road is rough, and the way is difficult—times of adversity. Jesus told us we could expect this, "In this world you will have trouble. But take heart! I have overcome the world" (John 16:33, NIV). Heaven will be different, but for now we each will have adversity and prosperity.

Ken gave up a good-paying job to become an executive in what seemed to be a growing, thriving corporation. He was now second man on the totem pole and had invested most of his own assets in the promising company. It was energizing—working for this enterprising multi-millionaire, drawing a generous salary, and whipping around in his plush business car. After nine months, Ken saw that the company was in deep trouble—cash flow low, credit shot, salary checks bouncing, benefits withdrawn. Uncertainty reigned for two years, and now the company has filed for bankruptcy. "We were so sure we were following in the will of God for us," Ken moaned. "Why did we ever get mixed up in such confusion? We have lost everything." He felt misunderstood, mistreated, and lied to.

Yes, there will be people in our lives who choose to go their own way, not God's, but that does not bind God's hands. He is still in control of the *people* who touch my life. He will work His purposes of good for me in spite of what they do. Remember, God's will for our lives is not that we live without suffering or hardship; it's that we become like His Son.

But what about Satan? Can God control him?

Job's String of Tragedies

Do you remember Job's story? The almost inconceivable events of Job's life all started when Satan came back from looking things over on the earth. From what we know of Satan in other scriptures, we can be quite sure he was up to no good—looking for someone he could accuse or tempt or discourage or deceive.[3]

It's as though God wanted to draw Satan's attention to Job when He said, "Have you considered My servant Job, that there is none like him on the earth, a blameless and upright man, one who fears God and shuns evil" (Job 1:8).

"Yes," Satan said, in effect, "I've considered him. I know why he serves You. It's because You're so good to him. If You hadn't blessed his work and increased his possessions, he wouldn't serve You. He would turn his back on You." It was as if the Lord said, "I know My servant better than that. He doesn't worship Me only because I am so good to him in supplying riches and material blessings. And to prove it, I will let you take these things away from him, *only you must not touch Job himself*."[4]

And believe me, when God gave Satan permission to do that, Satan took all the permission he received. Here's what happened.

One day when Job was going along with his regular activities, a servant came up to announce a tragedy. While that servant was speaking, a second servant announced a second tragedy. While he was still speaking, a third servant came along and announced a third tragedy. Job's camels, oxen, sheep, donkeys, and servants were stolen, burned, or wiped away in one way or another. Only a few servants escaped to tell the story. At this time Job was the richest man in all the East. The Bible records that he had over ten thousand animals and "very many servants." His riches were wiped out!

But that wasn't all. While the third servant was speaking, a fourth came with the most devastating news: Job's seven sons and three daughters were feasting together in a house when a big wind came along, blew the house down, and all ten children were killed.[5]

What do you think Job would *do* or what would he *say* when he heard the word of this incredible loss?

What would you do if only *one* child or *one* friend were killed in an accident?

Or, if your life's savings were wiped out?

Or, if even one small savings account were lost?

What would you do or say? Scripture tells us Job worshiped God![6] We, too, in the midst of a little or big crisis need to practice first remembering God and worshiping Him. Worship Him for who He is. He is so powerful that He can accomplish all that His wisdom, love, and goodness have planned. Therefore, even though I do not understand this which has happened to me or why He allowed it, I'll worship Him.

The Lord Gave—Did Satan Take Away?

Job's first words after he silently worshiped God were, "The LORD gave, and the LORD has taken away" (Job 1:21). Now wait a minute! Where did he get that idea? I thought it was Satan who took away everything from Job, didn't you? Yes, he did. He even used the Sabeans and the Chaldeans and the fire and the wind to accomplish his dreadful, destructive feat. Satan will always take the full length of the rope he gets! But don't forget, God put a limit on how far he could go, and he couldn't go any farther than that. The rope ended right where God said it would.

Job knew God was overall in charge. He knew something of God's name, something of His character, His attributes. Job was confident that God reigned. So, in effect, Job might have said, *Since God is all-knowing, all-powerful, and in charge, He could have changed things. But He didn't.*

You will notice Job did not say, "The Lord gave, and the Sabeans, the fire, the Chaldeans, or the wind has taken it all away." He does not even say, "The Lord gave, and Satan has taken it all away." Job looks beyond the people and events who happen to be the agents, to the God who sits above them all and is in control of all the agents involved. He acknowledges that the One who has taken away is the same as the One who gave in the first place. "The LORD gave, and the LORD has taken away." With these words Job acknowledged God's control.

Is Satan in the Circle?

Where then should we place Satan in our diagram? Can God do anything about Satan? Oh, yes! He belongs right inside the circle of God's control.

When Scripture tells us God is the Almighty One, it means precisely that. He is *all* mighty. Another scripture

says, "He who is in you is greater than he who is in the world." Who is the "he" that is in the world? Satan. Who is the greater one? God, the Holy Spirit.[7]

Even Satan recognized this. "Have you not put a hedge around him (Job) and his household and everything he has?" (Job 1:10, NIV). No doubt Satan would have loved to destroy Job, but knew he couldn't get through the hedge without God's permission.

Notice the limited permission God gave to Satan: "Very well, then, everything he has is in your hands, *but on the man himself do not lay a finger*" (Job 1:12, NIV, italics added). God opened the hedge around Job only so far—touch all that he has, but not the man himself.

So Satan went out and started his incredibly destructive work. The four tragic events happened which resulted in Job's losing all his riches and his ten children. But remember, Satan was limited. At this point, he couldn't touch Job himself. When Job blessed the name of the Lord, Satan wasn't ready to give up. "Yes, but if you strike his body—his flesh and bones—he'll curse you." Then God chose to give Satan permission to touch Job's body, *but not his life*. Satan once more went out and did what he could. But again he was limited![8]

God Is a Hedge Around His People

What a comforting truth! God has put a hedge around us, His people. Nothing good or ill and no one intending good or ill— including Satan, man, or events—can pass through that hedge to touch us except as God directs or allows.

This hedge is *not* a special force field that God puts around Christians to make us exempt from troubles. It doesn't shield us from the problems and sufferings inherent in a fallen world. But we can be sure that the trouble has passed through the permissive will of our loving Father before it touches us, regardless of the originating agent.

Psalm 125:2 expresses this same truth in another way: "As the mountains surround Jerusalem, so the LORD surrounds His people from this time forth and forever."

"Around the chosen city the mountains stood like sentinels, leaving no part without its barrier. So is God . . . round about us, . . . as an envelope to a letter, as the atmosphere to the configuration of our bodies. If then He chooses, He can pass off from us any arrow that might harm us; but if He opens His environing protection, so as to let it pass through to us, by the time it has traversed the atmosphere of His care, it has become His will for us. Put God between yourself and the entire world of men and things."[9]

Another significant dimension to our diagram, then, is this: God has put a hedge or mountains about His children.

The Atmosphere of God's Love

What happened to Job came to him through the atmosphere of God's loving care and protection. God allowed Satan to do some evil and destructive things, but God didn't close His eyes. He was still wide awake and nothing was out of His control, nothing was too much for Him to handle. He was filtering it all through His character.

God can never act contrary to Himself—to any of His attributes. Thus He filters all things through—

His love which is full of compassion,
His wisdom which cannot err,
His goodness which cannot fail, and
His power which cannot be restrained.

The ultimate result was for the good of Job himself, his family and friends—his "miserable comforters"—and for the glory of God.

Job is not the only scriptural example that shows how God opens the hedge and allows Satan's evil intentions and work to come through. Recall the "thorn in the flesh," the "messenger of Satan," sent to torment Paul. God allowed this to come through the hedge to touch Paul, and for a good reason which Paul recognized and accepted—to keep him from being conceited.[10]

Satan is real. He is mighty, but God is *almighty*. Sometimes God allows Satan to test and try His children, as He is in the process of accomplishing a greater purpose. Satan was allowed to test even God's own Son. At other times, God is more greatly glorified in preventing Satan from interfering. So, while we can rest assured that God is not intimidated by Satan, on the other hand we are told to personally resist him, his attacks and temptations. We are assured that the temptations that come to us will not be more than we can bear, for God delights in delivering His child from Satan's activity.[11]

Satan is evil in himself, and he incites men to do evil. Just as God doesn't *cause* Satan's evil activities, God doesn't *cause* men to do evil things—murder, rape, reject, envy, jeer. But He sometimes allows the evil of Satan or the evil or wrong choices of men to touch His children—with His full knowledge.

Satan has never sneaked around, unnoticed by God, to do his devastating work. How could we trust our concerns to God if, after all, Satan is allowed to spoil them without any restraints? No, God is wide awake and in control. Whatever Satan does—either directly or through his messengers—and what comes to us through people or events, is Father-filtered . . . past, present, future.

Hannah Whitall Smith explains it so clearly: "Second causes must all be under the control of our Father, and not one of them can touch us except with His knowledge and by His permission. It may be the sin of man that originates the action, and therefore the thing itself cannot be said to be the will of God; but by the time it reaches us it has become God's will for us, and must be accepted as directly from His hands. No man or company of men, no power in earth or heaven, can touch that soul which is abiding in Christ without first passing through His encircling presence, and receiving the seal of His permission. If God be for us, it matters not who may be against us; nothing can disturb or harm us, except He shall see that it is best for us, and shall stand aside to let it pass."[12]

All of Life Is Father-Filtered

Some of you may be thinking, "That's not my concern. My problem is my past. What about the sins I committed before I became a Christian?"

I have good news for you. God's control not only embraces the circumstances and people that surround our lives now, it also embraces the past. Pleasant or difficult, life hasn't happened by chance. Do you look back and say, "If only I hadn't married the one I married!"? Perhaps it *was* a bad choice, made in rebellion or infatuation. Or perhaps it was made with both of you seeking God's will, but it hasn't turned out to be what you had hoped for. Your spouse has turned against you or against the Lord or is creating difficulties you hadn't anticipated. Now, however, God begins where you are at the moment. Recognize that He permitted the union. He didn't *cause* it. You made the choice, but He permitted it. Possibly He even permitted your husband or wife to develop undesirable traits. These are a trial to you. God has had and still has control of the people and the situation as they now touch you.

God lovingly cares for you. Stewing about the past, fretting in the present, and looking anxiously into the future are all futile when you have a loving heavenly Father who is in control of all the people, events, and circumstances that touch your life.[13]

Whether you lose your job,
   the company dinner fails,
      it rains and your picnic plans are ruined,

your spouse becomes an alcoholic,
you discover you can't get pregnant,
your son breaks his leg playing
football, or
(fill in your own current situation),

determine to acknowledge that everything that happens in the humdrum or the crises of life is either directed or permitted by our loving Father who is wide awake and in control. Only our all-wise, all-loving, only-good God knows what is best, what will ultimately contribute to the good of His child in growing toward Christ-likeness. Hallelujah! Our God does reign and His reign includes everything and everyone that touches my life.

Throughout the Old and New Testaments we see clear evidence that God is in control. He is in charge of all things in the world of nature, nations, people, and events—even Satan.

"O LORD God of our fathers, are You not God in heaven, and do You not rule over all the kingdoms of the nations, and in Your hand is there not power and might, so that no one is able to withstand You?" (2 Chronicles 20:6).

"The king's heart is in the hand of the LORD, like the rivers of water; He turns it wherever He wishes" (Proverbs 21:1).

"For Yours is the kingdom and the power and the glory forever. Amen" (Matthew 6:13).

"Alleluia! For the Lord God Omnipotent reigns" (Revelation 19:6).

God is never unobservant. He never stands aloof with disinterest, nor does He wring His hands, help-lessly wondering what to do. He can and does intervene in the affairs of nations and people. And He is especially committed to His children who live the "listening

obedient" lifestyle. The earlier we learn to see life as filtering to us through God Himself, the earlier we will be
relieved from the stresses and anxieties that could otherwise plague us. Let's see what it means to trust the One
who has a master plan for our lives and works with this
bigger picture in view.

Making It Personal

1. What was Job's first statement after he heard of
the four tragedies that touched his life? In saying this,
what was he indicating he believed about God's control
of his life?

2. What is the difference between the person who is
only within the circle of God's control and the one who
is also living within the circle of God's will?

3. Another way of expressing that God is in control is
to say that He is sovereign. This speaks of His possessing
and ruling with supreme power and authority. Rightly
understood, no other truth about God can offer such
peace to the heart. How do these verses explain, describe,
or illustrate God's rule, authority, and sovereignty?

   1 Chronicles 29:11-14
   2 Chronicles 20:6 Nehemiah 9:6
   Job 41:11, 42:2
   Psalm 67:4; 75:6, 7; 95:3-5; 135:5, 6; 145:11-13
   Proverbs 21:1
   Isaiah 40:12-28
   Jeremiah 27:5
   Daniel 2:20-22; 6:26, 27
   John 10:27-29

4. What is Satan busy doing in the world now?

   Matthew 4:1, 13:19
   John 8:42-44
   Acts 5:3, 13:10
   2 Corinthians 2:11; 4:4; 11:3, 14, 15

5. How is Satan under God's control and what is his end?

John 12:31, 16:8-11
Acts 26:18
1 John 3:8, 4:4
Revelation 20:10

6. Satan still has God's permission to send his fiery darts at us (Ephesians 6:16), but God has provided us with full armor for our defense and battle. If the armor is in place, Satan cannot get through. What is this armor, and how does each piece enable us to repel Satan? See Ephesians 6:10-18.

7. How does God's truth (Ephesians 6:14) help in effectively fighting against these common fiery darts?

Evil thoughts: James 1:12-14, 4:7
Depression: Psalm 27:13, 14; 55:22; 103:13, 14
Fears: Psalm 27:1; 56:3, 4; 2 Timothy 1:7

8. God set a hedge around Israel that Pharaoh could not cross. How far could Pharaoh's magicians go in these instances?

Exodus 7:10-12
Exodus 8:16-19

How far could Pharaoh's army go? See Exodus 14:16-18, 23-31.

9. How does Psalm 105:13-24 further clarify the hedge God has put around Israel?

10. How did Jesus describe the hedge Pilate could not penetrate? See John 19:11.

11. What other pictures does God use to explain this hedge of His loving protection and providence?

Psalm 5:12, 31:20
Ruth 2:12; Psalm 57:1, 91:4

Psalm 18:2, Proverbs 18:10
Psalm 125:2

Choose one of these pictures that describes God's hedge about you. Mark it in your Bible and refer to it daily this week.

12. Copy the diagram on page 41. If your deep heart desire is to go God's way, write your name in the circle of "God's will."

Begin making a list of all the areas of your life over which God is in control. Divide your list into two parts: circumstances, people. Underline key words. Transfer these key words to the circle labeled "God's control."

13. Take one item from your list and have a meeting with God about it. Let it come through to you that God is indeed in control of this.

If we are in the King's road, at peace with the King, every stormy circumstance will be made to do us service. Yes, all our troubles will be compelled to minister to us, and to adorn us, and to make us more like the sons and daughters of a royal house. And, therefore, let us "joy in God." Don't let us be the King's own and yet march in the sulks! Let us march to the music of grateful song and praise.

John Henry Jowett,
My Daily Meditation

CHAPTER FIVE

The Bigger Picture: God's Master Plan

Much of my life in recent years has been spent catching taxicabs to airports and flying across the country to speak here and there. Sometimes those big birds don't move quite on schedule, and we have all kinds of unplanned situations. One morning, however, it was the taxi driver who was late. When I checked with the dispatcher, his answer was a cheery, "Yes, he's on his way; in fact, he's very close."

I said, "Thank you very much."

After waiting for quite some time, I called the dispatcher again. He reassured me that the driver was very close. "Thank you very much." After watching the clock tick off more minutes, on my next call I asked, "Could you tell me where he is?"

"Well . . . yes, . . . he's on 35th Place."

"Fine, that's very close. He should be here any minute. Thank you very much."

More minutes clicked past. Finally, we saw him come up over the hill, but he went right past our driveway. I ran to the phone again, "Sir, he's just gone past our house. Could you tell him he's on the right street? My friend will be out there to hail him in." He turned around, but again we saw him sail past.

The dispatcher and I were old friends by now. "Say," I continued, "if you don't mind, I'll just stay on the phone. When he is directly in front of our driveway, I'll tell you and you can tell him. (Pause.) He's coming now. He's slowly approaching. He's right in front of our driveway. Tell him to turn right."

With all this help, we finally got him into our driveway.

He sauntered up to get our bags. Since he seemed to be rather laid-back, I thought it my duty to share with him that we didn't have much time. "Sir, you know we're going to have to hurry because that plane is about to leave the ground."

Instead of getting at the business of putting the suitcases in the taxi, he looked at me and haltingly asked, "Well . . . ah . . . what time does your plane go?" I told him. "What time is it now?" I quickly told him the time. Instead of taking my word for it, he slowly got out his watch and tried unsuccessfully to see it in the dim light of the morning.

My stock of patience had run dry. With all the force my voice could carry, trying not to sound unladylike, I urged, "Sir, would you please hurry?" The tone in my voice was more than unladylike. But he hurried.

On the way to the airport, I noticed his breathing seemed unnatural. I could imagine many things—heart attack, asthmatic attack. Were we going to get to the airport at all? But that wasn't what I was most concerned about. I regretted my last impatient remark. My conscience was smitten. What do you do when you've spoken impatiently to a taxi driver—or to anyone? I knew what to do all right. I fly around the country telling women what to do, but it's hard when it comes to your own door.

As I turned to pay him for the trip, I knew I had a far more important debt to pay. So I said, "Sir, I am really sorry for the way I spoke to you back at the house. Would you forgive me?"

With his eyes on the bags as he shuffled them around, he replied, "Oh, that's all right, ma'am." His voice was subdued and kind and I knew he meant yes, he had received my apology.

Do you know why I got impatient with that taxi driver that morning? I had forgotten this truth which I'm writing about: God is in control of all things that touch me. My circumstances are Father-filtered.

God's Bigger Picture

My focus was on a narrow section of my own life. I was interested in keeping things on schedule. Now, there was nothing wrong in my creatively doing all I could to get the taxi there in order to get to the plane, in order to keep my scheduled appointment, in order to speak to the women in Illinois who were expecting me. I needed to take responsibility to do what I could, but, after doing that, I needed to recognize that this too was under God's control. I needed to rest in the fact that God sees the bigger picture and to trust that He is working events with that in clear view.

Perhaps we could illustrate it this way: Imagine the sky filled with ominous, black storm clouds. There is one that is darker than all the rest. Focus on that one. Now step with me into Psalm 104, verse 3, and I'll let you see the other side of the cloud.

"Who makes the clouds His chariot."

That black cloud turns out to be a chariot in which God rides. Looking at the dark cloud from God's point of view, it becomes a vehicle which is full of His presence, His glory, His blessing.

Now leave the cloud for a moment and think back to the last time your family put together a large puzzle. Maybe a thousand tiny pieces. There wasn't room to spread the pieces on one table. After they were all turned with the picture side up, you began with the obvious—the corners, the face of a man, a part of a large object. Most pieces by themselves had no meaning till they became part of the whole. Of course, you had the advantage of seeing the finished picture on the box.

As far as the big picture of our lives, God has that "finished sample" with Him in His chariot on the other side of the cloud. On our side, we have what He knows is better for us than seeing the whole picture—His promise: "And we know that all things work together for good to those who love God, to those who are the called according to His purpose." Though we may not see the good in a single piece, as He fits the pieces *together* over the years, they begin to fit into a *pattern for good.*

He knows where He's going in my life, and He's taking the best way to get there. My present heartache, financial instability, distressing family problem, or perplexing circumstance are simply pieces He allows in the puzzle. He knows just what shape pieces to fit in next. He knows and sees the bigger picture in regard to each individual circumstance in our lives, and He sees the bigger picture of the whole of our lives on earth and into eternity.

All God's Paths Are Peace

Before all the pieces were together, Naomi took it upon herself to pronounce judgment on God's ways in her life. The story is in the book of Ruth. "Do not call me Naomi (Pleasant); call me Mara (Bitter), for the Almighty has dealt very bitterly with me. . . . the Almighty has afflicted me" (Ruth 1:20, 21).

True, not everything in Naomi's life was good or pleasant, as we would judge it. Her husband and her two sons had died in a foreign land. One of her daughters-in-law had left her, and she had no material possessions. All she could see were the seemingly unpleasant pieces that didn't make sense.

Later, when the pieces came together, the puzzle became a beautiful picture. Dear Ruth was better to Naomi than seven sons would have been. Kind Boaz not only became their provider, but the father of Naomi's grandchildren. And perhaps best of all, Naomi was back in her own land, with her own people, nestling again under the shelter of Jehovah's wings.[1]

An indisputable fact (because it is in God's Word) is that God's ways are pleasant and all His paths are peace.[2] We may not have a sense of pleasantness as the pieces are going together, but the pieces have to be considered as part of the whole. Oh, dear one, let us believe that all His paths are peace as we wait in faith for Him to finalize all the pieces, working them together into a pattern for good.

Perhaps you can remember a time when you were perplexed and discouraged because God didn't answer your prayer in the way or at the time you expected. You were so full of faith. But it didn't come to pass. You may even have entertained the thought that God had forsaken you or at least didn't care. But now you can see what a fix you would be in if He had answered that prayer as you had asked.

Try to imagine with me what might have been in God's larger picture that morning when the only puzzle piece I saw was a late taxi driver and an airplane taking off without me. One thing I'm sure of, when I think clearly, is that God is more interested in my stockpile of patience than He is in my arriving on time in Chicago or Dallas.

Was there a message He wanted me to convey to that taxi driver? Could there be an accident He was causing me to avoid? Could He be teaching me to apply in my daily experience some significant practical truths so I could in turn teach others?

Give God Elbow Room

Our perspective is so narrow. We look for God to come into our lives in circumstances and events that please us. We would not put that dark piece of the puzzle in next. No, we say, let's work on this bright spot—it's so pleasant and cheery. Oswald Chambers says we need to give God elbow room. "Always be in a state of expectancy and see that you leave room for God to come in as He likes."[3] Give Him the right to be God in our lives.

Make room for God's surprise visits. It might be late taxi drivers. It might even be missing the plane. It might mean missing a night of sleep to meet my scheduled appointment. It might be far more intense trouble or suffering—the desertion of a spouse, the running away of a child, a broken engagement, a terminal illness, the loss of a loved one, a son dying with AIDS. Through it all, God is at work in our lives, wanting more than anything else to conform us to the image of His Son.

I met John when he was a freshman in the Christian boarding high school where I was Dean of Girls. During that year, he lived an exemplary life, but during his sophomore and junior years he rebelled and went his own way.

During the summer before his senior year, the Lord graciously dealt with him about his responses to authority and his lifestyle. Riding back to school with me that fall, he was expressing regret for his actions of the past two years. "I just feel terrible. Why," he moaned, "I feel I've wasted the past two years of my life!"

I listened till he finished and then realized he needed some practical help to start with a clean slate. We discussed the importance of his talking with the people at school whom he had wronged.

"Well, yes, I've talked to everyone—except for one teacher. I don't know what to say to her." So together we planned what approach he could take.

"Now," I said, "since you have done your part in asking forgiveness of those who were involved, it's very important that you don't let Satan come in to harass you and make you feel guilty about the forgiven past."

"Yeah, but two whole years wasted!"

"Didn't you say you wanted to have a meaningful ministry with people? You know, God is big enough to take some experiences out of these past two years and use them to help others. Why, He could even enlarge your ministry in the future through this. God is just that big."

"Yeah, but two whole years wasted!"

I saw that he wasn't going to get away quickly from the guilt and terrible sense of failure, so I pointed out, "Yes, but consider—when God had some important things to teach Moses, He took him to the back side of the desert for forty years. If it's only taken God two years to teach you some important things, look—He's saved thirty-eight years!"

His relieved grin told me he was on the way up. Twenty-five years later, he is still serving the Lord in a meaningful ministry to people.

God gives us some surprising promises for times when we feel we have blown it and all is a loss. Where we can see no way that this piece of the puzzle is working "together for good," He asserts, "I will restore to you the years that the locust hath eaten, the cankerworm, and the caterpillar, and the palmerworm" (Joel 2:25, KJV). Two years, six years, twenty years—wasted? "No," God promises, "I will reclaim for my glory those years that seem to you to be filled with useless rubble because of your failures." John needed to know that even the consequences of our own sins and failures are included in this precious promise.

He Gives Beauty for Ashes

With God there is forgiveness and restoration and beginning again. He says, "I want 'to give them beauty for ashes, the oil of joy for mourning, the garment of praise for the spirit of heaviness' " (Isaiah 61:3). Jesus knew ahead of time that Peter would deny Him, but He foretold Peter's tragic failure as a fact, not with condemnation. Then He took Peter from that failure into a ministry which has reached to every believer in succeeding generations.

We can depend upon God's super-abundant grace to transform our hurts, disappoints, failures, sins—even abuses—into benefits, our buffetings into blessings, our failures into comforts. That's grace! The transforming grace of our loving, forgiving, restoring Lord. He promises to transform the ashes into something beautiful and useful.

Heather was elated when she realized God was using something in her past to help someone else. "I was amazed," she explained, "to find myself admitting to a friend that I had been emotionally unfaithful to my husband in a friendship with another man some years ago. It is not something I talk about freely. Then I was surprised to hear my friend admitting that she was dealing with the same problem right now. I was able to listen and affirm her in how she is apparently handling it. I am thrilled that she felt safe enough to share her need with me.

"She is already doing well in removing herself from any opportunities to be with the man. We discussed several additional things she could do, such as using Scripture and meaningful songs to turn her thoughts to her Father's will for her. It seemed to be helpful to her. She does not *want* to get wrongly involved; her heart is right before the Lord, but she has that 'chemical reaction' like I have had with another man again even more recently. I understood her perfectly because I had walked that way before!

"It was so special to be able to let her know that I would love to help her be accountable in that area if she wants me to and that I am always available to listen when she's hurting. A 'divine appointment'? I believe it! And I'm grateful to be able to be a part of His kingdom work as He lets me minister to others every now and then through my past forgiven sins and mistakes!"

By His grace, God had transformed what seemed only a loss, and turned it to blessing for a fellow struggler along the way. The benefits spread in two directions.

Heather was thrilled that God was redeeming her failures and turning them into something useful in His purposes as she showed His compassionate love to another one of His beloved children. And it was such a help to her friend to have someone understand and pray for her—God's way of extending His arm of strength and showing His heart of compassion to a weak child of His.

So many wounded and hurting among us need to know that these same promises apply to those who have experienced all kinds of abuse. Some have had excruciatingly painful wounds inflicted upon them by the sins of others over which they had no control.

Finally, Someone Understands

Even as a preschooler, Elaine was quite a tomboy. With only boys for playmates, she could soon shinny up the highest tree as fast as any of the boys. "Our favorite project was building cabins," she recalled. "It was there that it happened—the thing that was to haunt me for years. In one of our cabins where no adults would ever see, I was raped by a young boy as the others watched! From then on I lived under the shadow of their threat, 'Don't ever tell or we'll beat you up.' And I knew they would. One of the rippling effects of that rape in the cabin was that whenever they 'wanted me,' I had to be at their disposal. It got to the point that I believed this was what men were for, and women are just 'there for them.' It gave me such a wrong view of men, even though I was so young.

"I couldn't share this with anyone and lived with a constant sense of guilt and overwhelming fear. I hated those boys and transferred that hate to my parents. My inner cry to them was, 'Why don't you ever ask me why I'm so unhappy, or why I'm afraid to play with those boys?' Or to God, 'Why don't you zap them with a piece of lightning or make this cabin fall down on them as punishment for this terrible hurt they caused me?'

"As my body began to mature, I knew it was wrong. I knew God wouldn't be pleased, but I couldn't deal with that either. It was a nightmare through my teen years. Many years later I was able to talk to someone and get help.

"But God! Yes, God is able to bring beauty out of the ashes of an unfortunate past. I have a deep understanding of anyone who has been abused this way. I feel their pain, and my heart longs to help them bring it to the surface and deal with it. For a number of years I counseled at summer camps. The young gals entrusted to me were often filled with hurts just like I had lived with. Because of my experience, I was able to be sensitive to their problems and in a caring and loving way help them to open up about it. When I would say, 'I know a bit of how you feel because a similar thing happened to me,' their mouths would drop open as they exclaimed, 'What a relief! Finally it's been told! And someone understands!' Later God also gave me an opportunity to counsel young women by phone while volunteering at our local Crisis Pregnancy Center."

Elaine is one more of God's precious transformations of His overruling grace. God has taken devastating experiences such as sexual abuse, a shattered marriage, financial collapse, or the wounds from growing up in a dysfunctional family, and turned them into something beautiful for personal growth and useful ministry. He can redeem bad situations, turning them into ministry in ways that are "far more than we would ever dare to ask or even dream of—infinitely beyond our highest prayers, desires, thoughts, or hopes."[4]

From the Other Side of the Cloud

Charles Stanley asks, "Is God really in everything? It is essential that we believe this truth, for it is the very foundation for faith. If God is not in sovereign control of your life as a believer—even when you disobey Him—then you have a limited expectation of when and under what circumstances you can expect God to be involved in your life. You must believe that even when you have disobeyed Him, God will use that for your ultimate good—consequences and all. (That is, of course after you get back into the line of obedience to Him and trust in Him, or back inside the circle of God's will.)

"If you will listen to God and believe His Word, Almighty God will take your difficulty, your heartache, and your trial and He will take the most disastrous situation, the most hopeless calamity in your life—and turn that thing around and show you that on the other side, yes, God can work good out of that too."[5]

What are you needing God's grace for now? The small frustration of an interruption? The confusion of things going "differently"? Or is it for a more crucial issue—sickness, pain, sorrow? Dare to affirm, though your feelings speak a contrary message, "I can't understand, but I can trust."

One old saint left us with this advice, "Meet every anxiety with the one short, sweet, strong answer—God! God will see to this. God will provide." That's looking at life from the other side of the cloud and realizing the cloud is God's chariot. God is coming to us in a special way in this incident.

God wants to conform us to the image of His Son, using us to minister grace to others, giving us strength for the journey and His stored-up goodness along the way. And all the tiny pieces fit into this larger goal, His finished picture.

These are the facts, but you've no doubt already discovered that simply *knowing* God is in control and that He has a master plan in mind does not necessarily spell heart peace. There's still a piece of the puzzle missing.

Making It Personal

1. What do we mean when we say God has the bigger picture in mind? What is He moving toward in our lives?

2. Beyond our small world, God's bigger picture also includes how we fit into His great world plan and purpose. What are some of the things this includes and how do they relate to us?

Matthew 28:18-20, 2 Peter 3:8-14
Psalm 67:1-7

His master plan also includes how we fit in with others. What do these verses tell us about this?

Matthew 5:9
2 Corinthians 5:18-20
Galatians 6:9-10
1 Thessalonians 5:11-15
1 Peter 2:13-15

3. How did Paul see his imprisonment as part of God's bigger picture which was working together for good? See Philippians 1:12-14.

4. What was Paul's attitude toward those who were preaching Christ with the wrong motive? Relate this to "all things work together for good." See Philippians 1:15-20.

5. How did God take what seemed only bad and turn it into something useful and beautiful in His purposes?

David: 2 Samuel 11:1-5, Psalm 51
Moses: Acts 7:22-36
Peter: Luke 22:54-62; John 21:15-17; Acts 2:14, 22-24, 37-41
Paul and Silas: Acts 16:19-34

6. Give some illustrations, either out of your own life or the lives of others, of how God brought forth

beauty out of what you or they felt were the ashes of past sins and mistakes.

7. This week, look for God's surprise visits. Don't put Him in a box, but let Him come to you as He chooses. Look for Him in each event and in each person you encounter. Make notes at the end of the day. Relate the events and people to Romans 8:28.

Who in My World Can I Trust?

The Lord must be the sovereign thought in my life. All true and well-proportioned living must begin in well-proportioned thought. God must be my biggest thought, and from that thought all others must take their color and their range.

John Henry Jowett,
My Daily Meditation

CHAPTER SIX

Restfully Sure of God's Loving Control

A few days after my routine annual physical check, the doctor called and said, "I have your lab report back, and there is something here that we need to talk about. I'd rather not talk over the phone. Could you come in this afternoon?" What was so serious that he could not share over the phone? I could make some pretty accurate guesses. My mind whirled.

As he put the test report before me, my kind Christian doctor gently spoke the word—*malignant.* Yes,

I would need to have surgery. I was quiet as he gave more details and asked if I had any questions. No, no questions came. As we sat silently, he asked, "How do you feel about this, Verna?" I replied, "Well, I really am quite shocked—there were no warning signs and no family history."

"I can understand that this has come as quite a surprise," he responded, "but you know, our God is sovereign and He really does love us and have our best interests in mind. Nothing comes to us except it passes through His hands first." In my mind I answered, *That's right, doctor. I know this is true. In fact, for years I've been teaching and writing about and attempting to apply these exact truths into the very edges of my life. Now I hear you saying I have a new opportunity to believe them in a crisis I've never before faced.*

It was as though these precious truths I have taught and which have brought comfort to me and to thousands of others were now being graciously handed back to me to get me through this new trial. Now the question was, would I believe them afresh for this new juncture in life? Or would the inevitable questions engulf my thinking: Will I be called on to suffer long and hard? Will death come sooner than I had ever imagined?

My Response to God's Loving Control

In any and every situation we can know God is in control. We can even believe He has filtered all things that come to us, that He could have changed things, but we can still choose to shake our fist in His face and through clenched teeth say, "God, I—don't—like—what—You've—done or what You've allowed to touch me."

The piece of the puzzle that's missing is my response. My *response* in difficult circumstances is of incredible significance. It determines whether I find comfort in the truth that God is in control, that He reigns in the circumstances which touch me, His committed child. My response determines whether I experience peace that passes understanding, or am bowed down with frustration, stress, pressure, unmanageable pain, resentment, and bitterness.[1]

Job's Words Reveal His Response

Let's look again at Job. After all those tragedies happened to him in just a brief span of time, we saw that he first worshiped God. Only after he worshiped did he speak. He spoke truth as his mind reviewed the facts, "The LORD gave, and the LORD has taken away." But his next words revealed his heart attitude as he added, "Blessed be the name of the LORD " (Job 1:21).

Blessed! In this one key word Job expressed his heart of trustful submission to God in the face of these disasters.

His focus was on the Lord instead of on the tragedies. His major focus wasn't even on the *hand* of God that allowed the situation, but on the "name of the LORD," the nature of God—that is, who God really is, His character, His attributes. Job chose to believe in God's wisdom, goodness, and love, as well as His power.

Job chose to bless God in spite of circumstances which seemed to contradict His character. He made a deliberate choice to trust God and praise Him instead of blaming or accusing Him. Job could have cursed the name of the Lord. He could have charged God with acting unwisely, or in an unloving way, or of being inattentive, unfair, tyrannical. Instead of choosing to believe these lies, he proclaimed, "Blessed be the name of the LORD." God's word verifies Job's attitude. It's recorded, "In all this Job did not sin nor charge God with wrong" (Job 1:22). Job chose to trust God during the impossible-to-understand happenings. This led to Job's acceptance of the situation.

Note that Job didn't thank God *for* the tragedies. He looked beyond what was happening and praised God for His character. Instead of shaking a clenched fist in God's face, Job's attitude was, "Even in this I know my God loves me and promises good to me. I don't understand, but I choose to trust!"

How Would I Respond?

As I drove home from the doctor's office, I realized I was at a crossroad. I knew some tremendous facts about God. Could I, like Job, rest in the Lord during adversity? What would be my response?

I called some friends to pray and then had to immediately fly off for another teaching trip. Back for a couple of days between trips, I went in for day surgery to discover the extent of the malignancy and to guide the doctors in determining the proper treatment. At the time, I had been studying about my Good Shepherd who feeds His sheep on green pastures. Why . . . this must be His pasture for me for this moment. If I will only graze upon it, trusting Him, I will find it a green pasture with all the needed nutrients for me to grow!

By God's grace I did choose to believe that my Good Shepherd is in charge:

He really does love and care for me.

He is selecting my pastures, and they are green ones.

He has proved faithful in the past, so how can I doubt Him now?

He has made no mistakes, and He is making none now.

As I laid aside my questions, He brought me to a place

of restful confidence as I chose to trust Him for what might lie ahead.

The day after the surgery, just before I was to leave again for a longer teaching trip, I received a call from the doctor, who was surprised to have the lab report back so quickly. His new announcement came as music to my ears, "There is no indication of malignancy!" Well, how do you explain that? Either the Lord performed a miracle of healing or there was a mistake some place. It really didn't matter too much at that point, and together we gave thanks to the Lord.

To be faced with an announcement which none of us wants to hear and thus be challenged to respond with trust was a good test.

Do I really believe God is in charge of all the conditions of my life, that He loves me, and that He is working for my best interests?

Will I, at this critical moment, choose to trust Him or choose to doubt these precious truths and promises?

Even though it was a short-lived valley experience, it taught me afresh the adequacy and faithfulness of our God.

In the face of possible loss, grief, and pain, we always have a choice: Are we going to choose to listen to Satan's temptation to curse God; to charge God with being unfair, unwise, unloving, unkind, inattentive, uncaring, or unable to do anything about it? Or are we going to choose to praise Him for who He is instead of judge Him for how He appears to be in this circumstance? Are we going to judge God by the circumstance which we can't understand, or judge the circumstance in the light of the character of God?

Response May Be a Process

This response isn't always easy. Sometimes it's a process. Often there's a struggle. A friend wrote, "Six months ago my husband was forced to resign his position because of deceit, lies, and false promises of some members of the Board of Directors who wanted their friend placed into my husband's job. My husband is a man of great integrity and had dedicated himself to service in this job.

"He resigned and I resented! I could not sleep at night thinking of the men who stood to gain by telling these lies. The bitterness haunted me and affected my children. It encompassed my entire life and conversation to the point where I had no ministry.

"I wanted them to fall on their faces. I longed for God to teach them a lesson! But life went on for them quite smoothly. I gloated over any bit of information which hinted that they might be having struggles.

"My husband now has a super job in a new town—a place we have dreamed about living and a job he feels great about. What more could we want? I should be writing these people thank-you notes for acting deceitfully in God's timing, but I am still thinking about how I can hurt them back.

"At your last seminar, Verna, I realized my need to forgive my husband's debtors and cancel that debt. I made that transaction with the Lord that day, but the battle continues. One man lives in a very large home by the river. I have to go by it every day to carpool my daughter to school. Satan is standing right there every morning, tempting me with new fuel for my resentment. Moving in a few weeks will help remove that temptation, but the real power is in the forgiveness and cancellation of the debt.

"It is so clear to us now that even in these bad things, God has been and will continue to fit everything into a pattern for good for our family, *as we respond rightly to the events and the people involved.*"

Whether immediate or recognized over time, this acknowledgment that God is over-all in control is essential for my response of heart surrender and confident trust. Such a response can be wrapped up in this one simple statement, "God . . . is the blessed controller of all things"—especially this thing that is touching me at this moment.[2] This is a concise way of not only acknowledging that God is in charge, but also expressing our acceptance of the situation and our trust in God as the *Blessed* One, the One to be praised.

GOD IS THE BLESSED CONTROLLER OF ALL THINGS.
(From 1 Timothy 6:15, Phillips)

I would like to recommend that you memorize this verse and bring it to mind in the thick of a crisis—little or big.

Inward Reaction to External Events

Through all the varied conditions of our lives, planned or permitted by our loving Father, His one great purpose is to hour-by-hour, moment-by-moment, conform us to the image of Christ. God wants to complete the good work He began in us at salvation. He promises:

He which hath begun a good work in you will perform it until the day of Jesus Christ (Philippians 1:6, KJV).

"Bishop Moule says the Greek word translated 'will perform it' means 'will evermore put His finishing touches to it.' Think of the fingers that made every lovely thing on earth, putting finishing touches to you and to me today. These finishing touches often come through the sweet joys of life, but they come, too, through the tiny trials, the little disappointments, the small things we hardly like to speak about, and yet which are very real to us. Let us think of them as the touches of His fingers—the finishing touches."[3]

Far more important to Him than giving us a life on easy street is the development of our character and our growth in grace. Every person and event that enters our lives moves toward that one all-consuming passion of His heart, that we be like His Son.[4]

The dynamics of this process are something like this. Nothing anyone can do to us can injure us unless we allow it to cause a wrong reaction in our own spirits. It's in this realm that growth in grace takes place. It's not what happens to me in life that is the most significant thing. It's my reaction to that external occurrence that fosters either peace or unrest within me.

It can be a simple thing like being irritated all night at the neighbor's barking dogs when I had hoped for a good night's sleep. I can react with irritation and impatience, adding more harm to my body and soul, or I can respond to God with acceptance. By this I'm not saying that acceptance means ignoring the problem if it continues. I'm saying the important thing is to make God my first reference and accept the situation, not with passive, fatalistic resignation, but with faith that He is working for my good. We may not control what other people or circumstances may do to us, but, by God's grace, we can control our response.

By God's grace none of us ever needs to be the victim of circumstances or ultimately damaged by the whims of anyone else. Instead, as we respond to God with acceptance—heart surrender and confident trust, even rejoicing—He will cause all things to fit into a pattern for good. He will cause even that negative thing to work for us. And, best of all, we grow in grace.

Jesus gave us the same challenge, "These things I have spoken to you, that in Me you may have peace. In the world you will have tribulation; but be of good cheer, I have overcome the world" (John 16:33).

Jesus has already overcome. My part is explained in those four little words in the middle, "Be of good cheer." Does that mean singing a happy little tune when your heart is aching? Is it mustering up a cheerful countenance for exhibition to the world? Is it being glad about the bad happening or difficult position we are in? No, it's saying in your inmost being, "Yes, Lord, what you're doing is okay with me. I recognize you as the Blessed Controller in this and I trust you."

Say aloud, as a way of confirming it to yourself and to Him, "God is the Blessed Controller of all things." When you make that choice, then, and only then, follows the heart-peace that Jesus promised here. Nothing can harm our spirits even in stressful times, as we respond in His prescribed way.

Paul's Thorn: A Divine Gift

Paul gives us a good example of a positive response to God in suffering (2 Corinthians 12:7). J. Oswald Sanders explains it this way:

"From his own costly experience Paul affirmed that his thorn was a Divine gift. 'There was *given* to me a thorn,' he says, and the thought behind the word is 'given as a favor'! True, Satan had a part in his testing, for he describes it as 'a messenger of Satan sent to buffet me' (v. 7). It was not God who instigated the test, but apparently, as in the case of Job, He permitted Satan to sift His servant, and by the time the testing thorn reached Paul, it had become not 'a messenger of Satan' but a gift of God's grace. It was given to him, not imposed upon him. What appeared to be the expression of the malice of Satan proved to be the beneficent gift of God, with a view to Paul's wider ministry. God's love is long-sighted. To Him the spiritual welfare and growth of His children is of far greater importance than their physical comfort; hence the ministry of suffering. He does not always spare present pain if it will produce eternal profit.

"Our personal thorn may be a physical limitation, a bodily deformity, a temperamental weakness, a mental handicap. To the great Dr. Alexander Whyte, the fact that he was an illegitimate child was a lifelong thorn, but how greatly it developed his sympathy and enriched his ministry! The main point for us is whether or not we have recognized in our particular thorn a gift of God's favor, or like Paul are endeavoring to thrust it from us.

"Once Paul perceived that the thorn he had been importuning God to remove was part of the Divine purpose of his life, his whole attitude changed. The world's philosophy is 'What can't be cured must be endured.' But Paul radiantly testifies, 'What can't be cured can be enjoyed. I even enjoy weakness, sufferings, privations, and difficulties.' So wonderful did he prove God's grace to be that he even welcomed fresh occasions of drawing upon its fullness. 'I gladly glory . . . I even enjoy'—my thorn."[5]

We have the choice: We can restfully accept our trials as being Father-filtered or turn bitter and let the resentment eat away at our spirits like battery acid eats through cloth. We can blame God, blame others, blame fate, but it will only end in ill-peace, misery, and a life wasted so far as usefulness to God's purposes in the world.

It is helpful to make a declaration of your faith as a response to God in any situation where you find yourself struggling with resentment, doubt, confusion. Something similar to:

> *Lord, I accept this happening in faith rather than in resentment and unbelief. I know you know what you're doing and whatever you allow to touch me is Father-filtered and comes to me out of your heart*

of love. I count this as another event in the 'all things' that you will work together for my good.

Making It a Life Habit

We need to learn to develop the habit of seeing God in everything that happens to us. And it *is* something that must be learned, a way of life that is to become a habit. So that in the midst of any little or big event in which I feel my world is falling apart, my first thought is of God, our loving Father. Whether or not we acknowledge Him makes all the difference in the world.

Let me illustrate what I mean.

It was October 15. My lap-top computer with its dead battery was at the repair shop, being readied for that magic date in late November when workshop travels would be over and I could settle down to the delicious joys of writing this book. Plenty of time to revive a simple dead battery, I mused.

But the repair shop neither had a battery, nor could they put one in if they had one, they reported. This was a factory job. And off the computer went to the factory.

Late November . . . my magic date came and went. Still no computer. Finally they reported, "A ship from Japan arrives December 7. We hope a battery will be on that."

I must admit I wasn't immediately seeing God in this circumstance. This company should have a greater concern for their name. After all, aren't they in a business where their success depends on satisfying their customers? And what computer-user doesn't want to use his computer now? At least they could provide a loaner!

Then my mind whirled for a solution. Where could I find a computer to borrow so I could get started on this planned project? Ron—of course! Good idea! He had a computer but no monitor yet. Gladly he brought his computer down to my office, connected my monitor, and discovered the computer didn't work. After trying everything he could think of, he took it in for repair. Waiting for that one would do me no good.

Perhaps I could take the large, less portable computer at the office home with me so I could work evenings and odd minutes. I lugged the thing home from the office to my study. Immediately it started doing strange things. The monitor light went out. The printer kept typing the same line over and over. Then the monitor gave a big pop, and the printer gave up all together.

After lugging the printer to the dealer, it was declared in fine shape. The computer dealer was baffled. Well, maybe it's the printer port. Bring everything! Computer, printer, monitor. A week later, still no computer. And two of my six golden weeks had already slipped into the past.

Then I realized I was so taken up with computers and the desire to stay on *my* planned schedule, I had forgotten to practice what I was in the process of writing a book about. Was God really in control of this whole business? Indeed He was!

Jehovah Shammah! "The LORD is there" (Ezekiel 48:35).

I needed to commit it all to Him. "O Lord, forgive me for my anxious thoughts, for my accusing thoughts toward 'them,' for my not trusting you in this. Help me to learn patience with sales people and repair departments, with people in general. Help me to learn to trust you with the timing of all events in my life. Help me to more quickly see you as the biggest factor in everything that touches me, and trust your unlimited love, unfailing goodness, and unerring wisdom. You make no mistakes. I acknowledge that computer problem came to me Father-filtered. You are my loving heavenly Father who is presently working for my best interests. Forgive me for my impatient spirit. Thank you for your loving concern. I will trust you."

A week later all three computers were out of repair and in working order. And the time seemingly "lost" will make no difference in eternity! Besides, I do have a pen that writes and a strong hand trained to use it. So what's all the concern about a machine—or even three of them—being in repair longer than the repairmen had said? But how I respond makes a great deal of difference in developing the grace of patience, which is Christ-likeness.

My Father Knows All about This

Though in my computer story I've used a rather minor delay and annoyance to illustrate the truth, yet we must follow the same principles in the major issues of life. God is omniscient and knows what is happening to us every moment of every day. He is the One who makes the final decision as to what can and what cannot happen to us. He is the great orchestrator—directing some things that happen to us and allowing others.

In my case He allowed each of the computers to have a problem. He allowed the computer people to be busy, delayed, or perhaps even neglectful. It is not that God planned it so that He could "teach me a lesson." But He did allow it and will use it for my good as I cooperate with Him.

By learning to appropriate these truths in the every-day minor crises, we are building a habit of walking in these truths, mentally bringing God into the situation and making Him our first reference and then viewing that incident, that trial, with the thought, "Why, my Father knows all about this. I will never think of anything He will forget. Why should I worry?" As the habit is developed and practiced, it will become a lifestyle—a natural response when adversities arise.

Seeing God in Everything

What is needed for true heart rest, then, is the habit of seeing God in everything and receiving everything that touches me as from His loving hands. The committed child learns to relate everything to his or her loving heavenly Father and receives the event as coming directly from the Father's hand—through His permission or direction—no matter who or what may have been the apparent agents, whether evil or good in themselves. This person believes that God is bigger than the adversity and will cause it to fit into a pattern for good. This response to the daily upsets of life is illustrated in the following note, written after a workshop I taught:

"Thank you for teaching us the truth that God is the Blessed Controller of all things. God has burned this into my life many times since the workshop. When I'm kept waiting for an appointment, my God is in control. When company arrives unannounced, my God can handle it and so therefore I can. When I've blown it and need to apologize so as to build my character, my God is in control. When everything falls down around me from diapers to in-laws to dreams, my gracious God is there to pick me up and put me above all of this.

"In the nitty-gritty of house remodeling He controls the time, the progress, even supplying the materials in a miraculous way. Knowing God is the Blessed Controller of all things has enabled me to see the light at the end of the tunnel. It has offered hope when there seems to be none. I've been able to tighten my grip and to hang on longer, and it has stretched my trust in God to a larger size."

This perspective is essential to experiencing a life of peace and joy. Mentally bringing God into the situation or seeing Him in everything that touches our lives is the only way we are able to respond properly when difficulties arise. It's the only way we can let our hardships and heartaches be a catalyst for our growth in grace.

Knowing that our God, the Blessed Controller of all things, is there, in charge, doing His work and fulfilling His promises releases us from resentments and from that which disturbs peace. But is it the cure-all for every conflict within? Does it end all my struggles?

Making It Personal

1. What is the faith statement that reminds us of Who it is Who is in control? Why is the word *Blessed* a key word? What does it express? (See pages 73 and 77.)

2. Explain the difference between responding to the Lord with a clenched fist or an open hand.

3. How did the Psalmist look upon his trials (afflictions)? From where did he acknowledge they came and what did he see them doing for him? See Psalm 119:65-72, 89-93.

4. From whom did Jonah receive both his troubles and his deliverance? See Jonah 1:17-2:10.

5. How can these verses help you to respond restfully to God's loving control? Write a key word or phrase for each response. Do you see any progression of response?

    1 Peter 4:12
    Jeremiah 11:5
    Matthew 11:26
    2 Corinthians 12:10
    James 1:2, Romans 5:3
    Revelation 19:4, 6

6. Obviously we cannot *actually see* God in everything. We *see* Him by faith (2 Corinthians 5:7). How do these verses help us understand what this means?

Romans 4:20, 21
2 Corinthians 4:16-18
Hebrews 11:1

7. Paul does not "glory in his weaknesses" and "take pleasure in his infirmities" because He is glad about the suffering itself, but about the end result. What is that? See 2 Corinthians 12:9, 10.

8. Let's take Oswald Chambers suggestion and "notion our minds that God is there." Make notes from these verses on God's presence and involvement in our lives.

Exodus 33:14
Deuteronomy 31:6-8
Psalm 139:1-12
Jeremiah 23:23, 24
John 14:16
Matthew 28:19, 20

9. What does it mean to make God your first reference? List some everyday events in which you can make God your first reference.

10. On pages 80-81 we have given a suggested declaration of faith in the Blessed Controller. It may be a help to you to replace the words "this happening" with a specific area of life that is overwhelming you right now. Let this declaration be your response to your loving Father this week as it relates to this one specific situation.

Peace, and even joy, are quite compatible with a great deal of pain—even mental pain—but never with a condition of antagonism or resistance.

H. L. Sidney Lear,
Joy and Strength

CHAPTER SEVEN

Does This End All Our Struggles?

Am I saying that believing the message of this book is that ultimate quick fix to end every struggle and mend every hurt? Will you have no need for more information, more challenge, more encouragement when you have read *this* book?

The answer is obvious. Realistically speaking, there is no one action we can take, no one truth we can put into practice which will put us on such a high spiritual plane that we will no longer feel earth's pains.

Today's typical western Christian is searching diligently and endlessly to find something to relieve and free him or her from the continual worries and hurts of life. We're always on the lookout for a quick fix for our mental, psychological, emotional, and physical pain. We go to classes or conferences. We read the latest book on coping. We talk to numerous counselors in our quest. And, if we are serious about our search, we carefully take the prescribed steps of action: exercise more faith, apply more diligence in studying the Word, pray more, spend more time in thanksgiving and worship, have more commitment, offer up more praise.

Having more of any of these good things may still not take away my soul anguish, my inner struggle.

We Are Made for Heaven

Realizing we are made for eternity will help us face our inner struggles. We're designed for a perfect environment, *but that isn't where we are now.* Right now we must live in a fallen, sin-infested world which is made up of an imperfect environment, imperfect people, and imperfect relationships.

In heaven, we are told, there will be no more death, no more pain, no more sorrow, and no more tears, but we aren't there yet. Jesus said, "Here on earth you will have many trials and sorrows" (John 16:33, TLB). As long as this earth has existed, people have suffered through troubles, trials, sorrows, and difficulties. Throughout the Scriptures we find that God's people suffered anguish and pain. They went through very distressing times in their physical world as well as in their own inner worlds.

For forty years in a desert, Moses had to deal with rebellious people, all the while struggling with his own feelings of inadequacy. The apostle Paul experienced an imperfect environment—shipwrecks, beatings, stonings, pain, prisons, weariness. Besides those outward struggles, there was the daily care of all the churches. *Imperfect people, imperfect relationships, imperfect environment.*[1]

Pain Has Purpose

It also helps us to face our inner struggles if we get a realistic view of suffering and pain, and understand some of its benefits. Philip Yancey, in *Where Is God When It Hurts?*, points out that physical pain is a gift from God for the protection and care of the body. It serves as a warning signal that something is wrong and needs attention.

Sometimes emotional pain alerts us to something wrong in our thinking or in our behavior. It's a warning signal that something needs to have attention or be corrected. So it can also serve to promote the health of the soul. Something in my life may be out of focus. For example, the pain of loneliness may be God's way of letting us know it's time to reach out to someone else.

Frustration may be a means of getting our attention and making us aware that there's something we can do to change our circumstances. A sense of invalid guilt indicates something needs to be corrected in my thinking.

Valid guilt shows us some sin in our lives that needs to be confessed and forsaken. I've slipped off track. As I let the pain tell me this, then I must do what is necessary to get back on the path of righteousness. (Confess sin and turn from it, recommit myself to the will of God, realize my need to depend on Him.) Our Father is gracious to help us get back on track in this way, even though it involves pain.[2]

However, our focus here is not on this necessary, though painful, conviction of the Holy Spirit in our lives because of sin. Rather, we will be considering other kinds of emotional pain. A loved one may die, and I grieve. A friend may turn against me, and I hurt. I may have been raised by alcoholic parents. I may have been abused as a child. This is different from the pain that comes when God is trying to get our attention. Inevitably, we will continue to experience emotional pain, suffering, and confusing struggles as long as we are on this earth.

Reconciled to the Reality of Pain

Pain *will be* with us during all our earth journey. Instead of resisting it with resentment, we can embrace it with hope. Or, as Phillips's paraphrase (speaking of trials) says, "Don't resent them as intruders, but welcome them as friends! Realize that they come to test your faith and to produce in you the quality of endurance" (James 1:2, Phillips). Once we have accepted the pain instead of fighting it, with the confidence that God will use it to draw us closer to Himself, we can move on and receive some of the tremendous benefits that can be ours as we let pain work for us—consciously walking with the Lord *through* our pain and struggles.

This doesn't eradicate the struggles, but it does minimize them. Instead of enduring a trial with self-depreciating thoughts or guilt feelings, or fighting it with a demanding spirit, we can accept and embrace it with the confidence that God will use it for good in our present lives and someday (perhaps not till heaven) fully deliver us. We can let the pain press us closer to the heart of Jesus and we will be richer in our experience of Him because of it. Even though our emotions are crying contrary messages, we can cry out, "Oh, the depth of the riches both of the wisdom and knowledge of God! How unsearchable are His judgments and His ways past finding out!" (Romans 11:33). I choose to trust Him even though I don't understand His seemingly strange ways with me at the moment.

For a number of weeks I struggled with pain in my heart at a time when I felt betrayed by a friend. One night upon awakening, it came to me that Jesus knew the grief of loss, the ache of betrayal, the pain of suffering. I recalled, "He is despised and rejected by men, a Man of sorrows and acquainted with grief" (Isaiah 53:3). And I realized that since Jesus was a man of sorrows and grief, He surely understood and felt my pain. It was all right that I felt sadness. He was betrayed and rejected and He is touched with the feeling of my infirmities.[3]

> "For to you it has been granted on behalf of Christ, not only to believe in Him, but also to suffer for His sake" (Philippians 1:29).

The Struggles of a Reflective Christian

The pain and struggle of life take on different forms with different people. Diverse personalities and temperaments will experience different struggles and varying degrees of internal suffering. The reflective Christian may struggle with questions about truth and doubts about God that others would not. Because of his or her very nature, he or she is bombarded with constant questions and can have some real struggles. A reflective temperament determines a basic approach to life—a perpetual pursuit of answers, but often not finding them.

Sally is one of these. "Verna," she confided, "do you remember when I told you with shiny eyes and deep conviction that I believed God was preparing me for something because my faith was so strong? I really thought I could handle anything He brought my way because of my unshakable confidence in Him and His goodness. I was right—there *was* a difficult experience coming my way, but I wasn't as prepared as I thought because through it I almost lost my faith!

"This test of my faith was home-schooling our children. Though it was a hard decision to make, I had had no doubts that God was leading us into it. Once the decision was made, I gladly gave myself to the task and trusted God to make a teacher out of one who was 'no teacher'!

"Four years and much bewilderment and disillusionment later, the kids are back in public school. I couldn't understand God's failure to come through—to enable me for the task I felt He had called me to. I felt I had trusted God to make me adequate as a home-school mother/teacher, even though I didn't really want to do it. And while committing myself wholly to Him, it seemed that He led me, running, into a brick wall.

"For years I was confused, hurt, and bewildered. If home-schooling wasn't God's will for me, how would I ever be sure of His leading again? Where do I go from here? And for the first time in my life, there was the terrifying thought that there might not be a God at all.

"These last few years, I have been driven to find answers for myself. Although there has never been a sudden illuminating experience that banished the darkness forever, there are now enough glimmers of light that I think I can go on with God. Only He is a different God than the one I thought I knew.

"I took a hard look at some Bible characters who must have been honestly confused. When Abraham was told to sacrifice Isaac, it flew in the face of everything he had learned about God. This longed-for, fulfillment-of-promise child who was the apple of his father's eye and the heart of his mother! How confusing it must have been to Abraham!

"And look at John the Baptist. Called by God from birth to prepare the way for the coming of the King of

all the universe. Living like an idiot and creating enemies everywhere because he was willing to go out on a
limb for his cousin, Jesus. And yet Jesus, who was now
doing miracles for others, seems to have forgotten the
loyalty of John and does nothing as John is imprisoned
and eventually beheaded. John was confused. 'Are you
really the Christ?' he asked.

"I saw no guarantees that we will live without
pain. The outcome of my sacrifices for God are not
always predictable. I may not receive back what I want.
I may be the epitome of the godly wife in 1 Peter 3, and
yet not only may my husband not change into the person I want him to be, he may divorce me. My children
may choose, as their father Adam did, to rebel despite
my good parenting, while the children of irresponsible
parents may be just what I would have loved mine to
be. Two plus two equals four in mathematics, but in life,
even the Christian life, sometimes two plus two equals a
bewildering five. Am I willing to serve this God who
confuses me? There is mystery in following God.

"Yes, there *is* 'joy in serving Jesus.' But equally true,
I need to temper the truth of 'Every day's a happy day
with Jesus in my heart' with reality so that I do not deny
the pain and confusion that I sometimes legitimately
feel. Nearly all the great saints of the past talk about 'the
dark night of the soul,' when God seemed far removed
and answers didn't come. If I want the spiritual matur-
ity that marked their lives, I need the grace of endurance
to forge ahead through the blackness. When I can see
the outcome, that isn't faith. Faith begins when I can no
longer see, no longer understand.

"Probably the greatest relief came to me when I
read the statement from Larry Crabb, 'God is most fully
known in the midst of confusing reality.'[4] I wasn't sure
what it meant, but suddenly I felt accepted in my confused state and even hopeful that life was not empty.

Maybe I was confused about who God is, and what He will and will not do for me. Maybe I needed to adjust my view of Him.

"Through this ordeal I have come to realize that what I thought I had before really wasn't faith. Now I know only that I don't know very much about God, but I do *believe* He will not allow me to suffer what I cannot bear. I also believe I don't understand what He means by that, and I may be called to live with the seemingly unbearable in obedience and trust without foreseeable resolution. However, I also believe He is good, because even while we're bearing the unbearable, there will be touches of love that can only come from Him."

Pain Comes from Many Sources

In addition to the struggles of the reflective Christian, there are many other kinds of pain and struggle, such as the pain that comes as a result of the death of or the clear rejection by a friend or spouse of many years. Though the experience may have pressed us closer to the Lord and taught us many precious and valuable lessons, there is still the ache in the heart because of the hurt and the tremendous sense of loss. Even the memory of good times together in the past brings pains and struggles and sometimes even brings back some of the unanswered questions. The deep hurt and intense pain are there and will not go away. To feel pain doesn't mean I'm not trusting adequately.

To continue to feel hurt, pain, and struggle as we live without these very significant relationships is not wrong or unspiritual. But, of course, if we let these feelings lead us into resentment, anxiety, self-pity, or even self-accusation, then they are wrong and need to be confessed and properly dealt with. Hurt, pain, and struggle are a part of the human condition, an inevitable part of living in this imperfect world.

Another might wrestle with the struggles that emerge from his or her own weaknesses, inadequacies, failures in spiritual life or in duties performed. It might be the mother whose child has departed from the way of righteousness. Her pain is especially strong if she feels there is something she did that was not wise or something she could have done—if only . . .

There is pain brought on by the loss of respect, expressed through belittling, insulting, ignoring, and abusing. Some live with this daily. Many spouses continually demean their partners. And one only has to keep his or her ears open in the grocery store to hear the painful belittling of little ones.

There is also the pain brought on by one's own mistakes and sins. A friend was telling how she came to realize she had hurt many people by her perfectionistic standards for herself and for others who had helped her on committees or even in simple projects. She cried hard as she expressed her painful memory of hurting instead of loving.

"I believed it was most pleasing to the Lord to get the job done right," she explained. "I wanted to please Him so I saw to it that the job was done right. Believe me, I was usually always able to present Him a perfect project. But," with excruciating pain evidenced by the tears in her eyes and trembling voice she said, "I didn't realize until recently that I have left behind in the wake a stream of wounded, hurting people. Now I realize what really pleases God is for me to show His love to people, and not to present Him with a perfect project. Is it possible for a woman with forty-five years of such habits to change? Yes, I'm sure it is because God is showing me more and more of His grace and He is changing me."

Until rather recently my ninety-one-year-old dad has had two good eyes. Now, however, he has been declared legally blind. He finds it very difficult to read anything or even to find the line on the check for his signature. This hard-working farmer, now living in a retirement home, has always been very active—work was his life. From the farm, he went to woodworking at age eighty. Then, losing his sight, he could no longer use the electric saw. At eighty-eight he learned to weave carpets on a large loom. He takes great pride in that and feels so good that he has something useful to do.

But now he is facing the fast-approaching time when he will not even be able to work the loom. Daily, there is reminder of the increasing loss of his ability to be active, to do something useful. This is a pain that will not go away. Further inability and loss will just increase as time goes on.

In many of these diverse conditions, we need to appropriately work through the grief, the forgiveness, the self-understanding. Or sometimes it might mean humbling ourselves to do all we can to mend a relationship. Yet many times even these proper actions will not eradicate the pain. A residual pain lingers.

Though He does not promise to wipe out the pain, Jesus assures us He will give overcoming grace as we continue to experience the real pain. The struggle may continue, but we can have hope and peace in the midst of the struggle.

In dealing with the pain, it is helpful to discern what is the real cause of our struggle. Is it a result of the inevitable suffering we feel as a part of a fallen world? Or is it due to a failure to trust the Lord because we don't really know who He is and how He feels toward us?

Making It Personal

1. Define *pain* as we are using it here.

2. What are different kinds of pain or struggles various people might have? What are some benefits of pain?

3. What are some things we may expect as we live in an imperfect world? Think this through on your own, then with the verses here.

2 Samuel 18:33-19:1
Psalm 41:9; 109:22; 143:3, 4
Proverbs 14:20, 19:13, 26:22, 29:22
2 Corinthians 11:24-30
James 4:13, 14

4. What can we look forward to in heaven?

Romans 8:17, 18
1 Corinthians 2:9, 13:12
Hebrews 4:9, 10
1 Peter 1:4
Revelation 21:3, 4, 22-27; 22:3-5

5. However, we are not left alone with our struggles now. There is help and hope in Jesus Christ and His written Word. What does He promise for times of:

Loss of respect (belittled, insulted, ignored, rejected, etc.)? See Deuteronomy 10:17, 18; 1 Samuel 12:22; Psalm 9:9, 10; 59:9, 17; Isaiah 49:15, 16; Romans 8:31-34.

Personal weakness and inadequacy? See Psalm 27:13, 14; 37:23, 24, 39; 43:5.

Material need? See Psalm 102:17; Habakkuk 3:17, 18; Matthew 6:31-33.

Grief? See Psalm 23:4; 30:5; 1 Corinthians 15:20-22, 55-57; 2 Corinthians 5:1-4.

Physical weakness? See Psalm 41:1-3, Proverbs 4:20-22.

Growing older? See Psalm 23:6, 37:25, 92:12-14; Isaiah 46:4.

6. How did these deal with their pain or struggles?

Hannah: 1 Samuel 1:1-18
Paul: Philippians 1:29, 3:10; Colossians 1:24

7. How do these verses express God's promise to give the grace of endurance?

Isaiah 40:29-31
Philippians 1:6
Hebrews 12:1-3
James 1:2-4
1 John 5:4, 5

8. How can pain press us closer to Jesus?

Psalm 119:67
Isaiah 26:16

9. Was there anything in Sally's testimony that helped you in a personal struggle?

10. Is there a lingering pain or hurt in your life right now? Can you find verses from question five that you can use as your anchor of faith?

How can we measure God's love? They say that a man's fist is the measure of his heart. Come and stand beneath the stars! There is God's hand! Now judge His heart! It is illimitable! By that love He has put our sins behind His back into the ocean depths! Through that love He will bring us to glory! His is a love that will never let us go!

F. B. Meyer,
Our Daily Walk

CHAPTER EIGHT

Why Do I Find It Hard to Trust God?

Eight-year-old Andy eagerly sidled up to his mother, "Mom, can we go to church camp again this summer?" "I don't know, Andy," Mother responded, "let's pray about it." Andy's shoulders drooped as he shuffled away, "Oh, no! If we pray about it, I know we can't go!"

Sadly, Andy had a wrong concept of what God is like. However, not only children, but many adults also, have wrong ideas about God. "I have a dreadful fear of failure," a young man confided, "and I always felt, whatever I did, that I could have done it better. It was all tied to my upbringing which was legalistic and perfectionistic. The message that came through to me was, 'We love you when you succeed; if you fail, we don't love you or accept you.' I believed this, not only about my parents, but I transferred it to other people and to God. God would only love me if I lived up to His expectations—which were way beyond what I could do."

Wrong concepts of God keep us from being comforted by the God of all comfort and hinder us from trusting Him who is worthy of our trust. As long as we have doubts about God's goodness, we can't find comfort in the truth that everything that comes our way comes from Him, that it is, in fact, Father-filtered.

So before we attempt to answer in some small measure the question, "What is God like?" let us uncover some of our blind spots, some of our unconscious ideas about what God is like. What we actually think God is like and how we think He feels toward us is one of the biggest reasons we don't draw close to Him and find our security in Him. That's one of the reasons we struggle. We don't *really* know Him. And most of the time that's why we find it difficult to trust Him.

Judging God by One Event

Often we single out an experience and say, "If God is really God, why doesn't He do something about all the pain and problems of the world?" Or, "Look at the death and destruction which the San Francisco earthquake brought. You can't tell me God really *cares*."

Just as we read wrong motives into the actions of people through one isolated incident, we do the same with God. I remember one time when I did this while I was Dean of Girls at a Christian boarding high school. As I walked toward the room where we gathered for morning staff prayer, I was glad to see Leanne standing at the door where I had to enter. Her daughter was under my care as a student and just that week I had had to administer some discipline that the faculty had assigned to her.

Leanne and her husband had always been supportive and understanding of any past dealing with their daughter, but it was always so good to have a contact after such an action to know that all was well. As I approached the door, hoping to have a moment with her to smile and say a friendly word, to receive a smile and sense of acceptance back, instead . . . she turned her back to me.

Oh, no! She does feel the correction was unjust. She's avoiding me! The coolness seemed to continue for days. Finally, one day she was in her classroom alone, and I decided to speak to her about it. As she saw me approaching, she looked up with a big smile and exclaimed, "Well, Verna! I just want you to know that my husband and I really appreciate you." Appreciate me? That wasn't what I expected to hear nor what I had been reading in her behavior those past three days.

I had misread her actions and her attitude toward me. It all began when she turned her back toward me at one strategic moment. It blocked out all I knew of our past good relationship. It made me uncomfortable and gave me three days of agonizing over a problem that wasn't even there.

Whether consciously or unconsciously, we sometimes read into a single action of God toward us motives and attitudes which are not His, but only our dreamed-up ideas. We can't base our understanding of God—or anyone—on one event. We can wonder why God allowed it, but if we focus on that isolated situation, we forget all of His past goodness and the promise of His lavish new mercies for tomorrow.

Allowing God to *be* God is hard for us.

Letting *Him* call the shots.

Letting *Him* order our circumstances in His providential sovereignty.

Being satisfied with *His* choices.

Accepting devastating events without demanding an explanation.

So from our limited view—drawn from one event—we perceive that God is unkind, unwise, uncaring, or unable to do anything to change the situation.

We Compare God to Imperfect Humans

Like the young man at the beginning of the chapter, many of us think of God as being like people. A friend told how her mother and step-father would *send* her and her brother to Sunday school and church just to get them out of the house. "They wanted to get rid of us, so Saturdays we were sent to the movies, Sundays to church. Thinking about God in church was awesome to me. I never saw anything at home that helped me relate what they were saying at church. They said, 'God is like your father.' My father was very strict, harsh, and unkind, so I assumed God would be the same—getting after me for the least thing I did, yelling at me, and threatening with unkind words. I trembled because I knew I didn't measure up so I expected God to zap me or punish me at any moment."

We tend to think that . . .

God is a busy, uninvolved parent: "He's too busy and doesn't have time for me. People don't have time for me; God doesn't either. He has the whole universe to care for. I shouldn't bother Him with my petty concerns and needs."

He will fail as people do: "He will fail me just like everyone else. How could I possibly be important enough for Him to take an interest in? He is no different from the people who have failed me."

He doesn't understand me: "I have unique problems that He does not understand. I'm the exception—my weaknesses, my temperament, my terrible background. I'm different. He doesn't understand me."

He is a partial parent: "He's good to others, but He isn't good to me. Good things always happen to Mary, but things like that don't happen to me."

He is an accusing parent: "He is a harsh judge and enjoys making me feel guilty and miserable when I do wrong. He just waits to punish me at the first slip."

I should be strong enough on my own: "It's a weakness in me if I have to go to God with my needs. I should be strong and be able to handle life on my own." One woman said that her father taught her that to go to God in a time of need was a sign of weakness.

God is a perfectionist parent: "I have to earn His favor. I feel I must earn His love by being good, by increasing in my prayers and Bible study. I'm afraid that I'm not quite good enough for Him to give me that desired blessing."

People have disappointed us, betrayed us, used or abused us, and we cannot trust them. We tend to make God out of the same mold and materials. Many times these impressions come from the way our parents have treated us or are implications drawn from our experiences with them or other authority figures. But God is vastly different from what we are, even the best of us! God is limitless in His love toward us. He is enormously patient and longsuffering. He knows no growth, nor does He diminish in anything that He is because He is complete. We are the opposite. We finite beings can't possibly fully comprehend Him.

" 'To whom then will you liken Me, or to whom shall I be equal?' says the Holy One" (Isaiah 40:25).

We must forever put away likening God to human beings, unless we are pointing out a godly quality in someone who is fleshing out the fruit of the Spirit and saying, "God is like that, only much more so." The only person who shows us what God is really like is Jesus Christ who came to reveal the Father.

"The Son is the radiance of God's glory and the exact representation of his being" (Hebrews 1:3, NIV).[1]

J. I. Packer, in his classic, *Knowing God*, expresses it this way: " 'Your thoughts of God are too human,' said Luther to Erasmus. This is where most of us go astray. Our thoughts of God are not great enough; we fail to reckon with the reality of His limitless wisdom and power. Because we ourselves are limited and weak, we imagine that at some points God is too, and find it hard to believe that He is not. We think of God as too much like what we are."[2]

Hannah Whitall Smith, in *The God of All Comfort*, acknowledges this same malady. "Because we do not know Him, we naturally get all sorts of wrong ideas about Him. We think He is an angry Judge who is on the watch for our slightest faults, or a harsh Taskmaster determined to exact from us the uttermost service, or a self-absorbed Deity demanding His full measure of honor and glory, or a far-off Sovereign concerned only with His own affairs and indifferent to our welfare. Who can wonder that such a God can neither be loved nor trusted?"[3]

We can readily see that these ideas are diametrically opposed to what Jesus Christ was like. Jesus came to reveal the Father. He was God "manifest in the flesh." We see in Jesus the "express image" of God. Anything that is contrary to the life, words, and ways of Jesus is not true of God the Father.[4]

Taking a Stand on Truth

After becoming aware of the wrong ideas we have had about God, we need to consider what He is really like and deliberately choose to believe what God says about His person, what He tells us He is like.

One way to do this is to read through the Gospels, taking special notice of what Jesus is like—His manner, His feeling toward people, how He treats the weak and the sinful. Make notes of what you find and review these periodically.

It would be an added help to write out a declaration, "No matter what seems to be, nor what my own thoughts and feelings are, nor what anybody else may say, I know that what Jesus reveals about God the Father is true, and I will not let myself think of Him in terms of these wrong thoughts or ideas. When the temptations come to think wrongly of Him, I will rehearse and remind myself what God's Word tells me He is actually like."

If we are going to experience the comfort of God's blessed control, we must learn what kind of Father He really is. We need to deliberately and consistently take a stand on the truth about Him.

To have thoughts and questions and doubts about the person of God *so as to think through issues* can be a very healthy exercise which leads to a more solid faith. As I said earlier, to be *tempted* to question God's goodness is not wrong; it may simply be a part of the human condition or it can also be from Satan. However, even when the temptation comes from Satan, the temptation itself is not sin. Jesus was tempted by Satan, yet He did not sin.

Habakkuk, the Psalmist, and John the Baptist all had questions, but they brought them to God.[5] What we do with our questions and doubts on a continuing basis is what we are addressing here. When our questions become charges against God that He is different from what He tells us He is and lead to bitterness because of it, they become destructive and eat away at our inner being like cancer.

It's possible to embrace the truth about the character of God, but still have some feelings of wonder, frustration, confusion, and struggle. We shouldn't deny or stuff our feelings. But to have feelings of resentment toward God for not changing things or answering our prayer in our way and time is a sinful reaction that keeps us from peace. *Those* feelings need to be dealt with.

We need to take captive the wrong thoughts of God that do not line up with the truth and to bring every thought to the obedience of Christ.[6] As we discard wrong thoughts and replace them with true thoughts about God, we will find that our minds and hearts have a different outlook. This is what Romans 12:2 calls "the renewing of the mind." It is an on-going process and is not accomplished in a day!

Talk to Yourself about God

We need to come to know God as He truly is—cultivating a deeper relationship to Him, and enlarging our personal acquaintance with Him. Not just know more *about* Him, but come to *know* Him. How is this to be done? Packer answers the question in this way:

"The rule for doing this is demanding, but simple. It is that we turn each truth that we learn about God into matter for meditation before God, leading to prayer and praise to God. . . . It is a matter of talking to oneself about God and oneself; it is, indeed, often a matter of arguing with oneself, reasoning oneself out of moods of doubt and unbelief into a clear apprehension of God's power and grace."[7]

David, in many of his psalms, practiced this talking to himself. "Bless the LORD, O my soul; and all that is within me, bless His holy name!" (Psalm 103:1). If David were living today, his words might sound something like, "Don't you forget, soul of mine, it is God who forgives and heals and redeems, who even fills your life with His lovingkindness and satisfies you with good things. This, David, is what your God is like. Bless Him! Praise His name!"

The Psalmist even puts into words what he knows God to be like:

"For You, Lord, are good, and ready to forgive, and abundant in mercy to all those who call upon You" (Psalm 86:5).

"O LORD God of hosts, who is mighty like You, O LORD? Your faithfulness also surrounds You" (Psalm 89:8).

"I will say of the LORD, 'He is my refuge and my fortress; my God, in Him I will trust' " (Psalm 91:2).

On the other hand, David also brought his honest doubts and questions and voiced them to God. Psalm 22 continues for twenty-one verses with a complaining plea for the Lord to see his dire situation. But in verse 22 he breaks out in praise that God has heard, the kingdom is His, He is to be praised. When the questions lead us to the truth about God, the questions are good, providing a catalyst for growth.

Continuing to affirm our need to know God, J. I. Packer writes, "I know nothing which can so comfort the soul; so calm the swelling billows of sorrow and grief; so speak peace to the winds of trial, as a devout musing upon the subject of the Godhead. . . . The world becomes a strange, mad, painful place, and life in it a disappointing and unpleasant business, for those who do not know about God."[8]

Knowing God is the believer's lifelong pursuit. We turn now to a brief look at our loving, compassionate God who is worthy of our trust.

Making It Personal

1. Review the wrong thoughts about God that many people typically have (pages 99-100) and ask God to make clear to you which of these ideas you have been unconsciously entertaining. If you don't identify with any of these, in a quiet time of thoughtful meditation and prayer, ask the Lord to reveal to you any misconceptions that you may have.

2. Write out your own words or a specific Scripture verse that will refute those wrong thoughts with God's truth. Do this for each one that you have listed. For example, Psalm 145:9, "The LORD is good to all," would help in refuting, "God is like a partial parent."

3. Read Psalm 77. List some of the troubled feelings and questions Asaph, the Psalmist, expressed. Where does he begin to change his way of thinking about God? Can you trace how he reconciles his thinking?

4. Is it possible to embrace the truth and still feel what you feel? *How* can one do this without denying his feelings?

5. What is our counterattack from the Word of God when we are tempted to think of God as:

Unfair: Deuteronomy 32:3, 4; Psalm 96:10; John 5:30
Unwise: Daniel 2:20; Colossians 2:2b, 3
Unloving: Romans 8:35-39, 1 John 4:16
Unkind: Psalm 117:2, Isaiah 54:10

Inattentive: Psalm 55:16, 17; 1 John 5:14, 15
Uncaring: Lamentations 3:22, 23; Matthew 9:36;
    1 Peter 5:7
Unable: 2 Corinthians 9:8; Jude 24

6. From these psalms, write down each word or phrase you find which describes God's character: Psalm 25, 36, 47, 86, 89, 111, 145.

7. Jesus said to Philip and His disciples, "He who has seen Me has seen the Father" (John 14:9). He said the works that I do, the words that I speak, the life that I have is of the Father. To consider what God is like, go through the Gospels and answer the question, "What is Jesus like—what was His attitude toward people and His way of dealing with people?"

Here are a few verses to help you get started in answering those two questions about Jesus:

Matthew 9:36, 15:32; Hebrews 4:15
Mark 10:43-45, Philippians 2:5-8, John 13:13-15
John 14:1-3, 27
Mark 2:15-17
Luke 4:18
Matthew 8:23-27, 28:18

8. Based on your study in the Psalms and of Jesus, spend time praising God for who He really is.

9. Sing a song or chorus that praises God for His attributes, for who He is. Or make up your own words for a song tailor-made for your need.

Once, when staying in the country with a friend, he took me into his garden and showed me the weather-vane over his coach-house, and asked if I could distinguish the sentence woven into its texture. I discovered it to be: "God is Love!" "Yes," he said, "for I have found that whatever comes to me is from the quarter of the Love of God!"

F. B. Meyer
Our Daily Walk

CHAPTER NINE

Does God Really Care About Me?

To live successfully in this strange, sometimes unpleasant and hurtful world, we need to know our God is trustworthy. We need to have personal acquaintance with His sympathetic, compassionate nature. We do this by pondering the various aspects of His person.

More than anything else, we need to discover for ourselves the love that God has for us. I say 'discover' because His unfailing love for us exists, whether we know it or not, but we do not enjoy the comfort of it unless we discover it for ourselves. There is no reluctance on His part to reveal His love, and we may have the joy of continual discovery. In doing this, we are developing the habit of meeting all our difficulties and anxieties, all our fears and perplexities with the solid, eternal truth of God's loving care for us personally.

> "They who know Your name [who have experience and acquaintance with Your mercy] will lean on and confidently put their trust in You" (Psalm 9:10, AMP).

God's Love Is Free, Unprompted

We have friends who love us. In her long, regular letters, my friend Rachel keeps emphasizing that she doesn't want me to feel obligated to her. She just counts it a privilege to pour out her thoughts and feelings to me on paper. She considers it an honor if I take time to read the epistles, feel concern for her, and pray for her. She doesn't make me feel guilty nor does she demand a certain response from me. She loves me *freely*.

Can you believe I love her? Yes, I love her because of who she is, but I also love her because of how she feels toward me—she loves me and she expresses it so caringly!

That's the way we humans tend to love. Something in the other person prompts us or draws us to love him or her. Our spirits connect. We love the person.

Too frequently we think of God's love for us as being similar to our love for one another, but His love is vastly different in origin. God's love for us originates in Himself. It is a self-caused, free, unprompted love. There was nothing whatsoever in a single one of us that called forth or prompted Him to exercise His love toward us. His love is simply an expression of His great heart of love for us. "The LORD did not set His love on you nor choose you because you were more in number than any other people, for you were the least of all peoples; but because the LORD loves you" (Deuteronomy 7:7, 8).

Actually it's even more than coming from His heart of love. The Scripture says, "God is love" (1 John 4:8). Since God *is* love, it's a part of His nature to spontaneously, freely love with a love that encompasses each one of us personally and individually no matter how unlovely we are or feel ourselves to be.

God's love doesn't depend on whether we measure up to certain expectations, or whether we have given a proper response to His love. Nor does He portion out His love according to our devotion to Him or according to our successes and failures in living a godly life. Or even according to the hours we spend in prayer or reading the Word.

To me, this *free, unearned, unprompted* love of God is one of the most comforting and rest-producing truths in Scripture! If I know that nothing in me or in my behavior drew out His love for me, then nothing I am or am doing or ever will do will cause Him to love me less or turn His love away from me. His love is unconditional, measureless, limitless.

Of course, there are some requirements, some conditions that will determine whether I *sense* His love for me, whether I am able to receive comfort in His love for me. When I sin against Him—disobey Him—I put up a blockage so that I can't sense His love coming through to me. I will not *feel* His love, but God has not changed. He still loves me. It is I who have changed and I need to change again.

When I sin against Him, before I can again experience the comfort of His love for me, I must repent, confess my sin, and turn back to Him. But even if I don't repent, His love won't be taken away from me. Nothing I say or do—or don't do—can change the fact of His love. [1]

Everlasting, Undiminishing, Complete Love

God loves us with an everlasting love. Since He has loved us from eternity, before time began, His love would have to be self-generated. There couldn't possibly be a cause in the person to draw it out, because that love was in God's very nature from before people existed.[2]

He loved us when we were loveless and before we had a particle of love for Him. That love couldn't possibly be influenced by anything we are or do. It has always been what it is—even before our time. And since it is everlasting, it will never, never be diminished one iota by our behavior or our performance, by any of our thoughts or deeds, or lack of them.

Likewise, His love can't grow any greater. It is as great, vast, and deep as it could ever possibly be. I can go deeper into the comfort of His love for me, but His love itself will not change—it's perfect and complete from the beginning.

What a tranquilizer for the heart!

This, this is the God we adore,
Our faithful, unchangeable Friend,
Whose love is as great as His power
And knows neither measure nor end![3]

In all the varying circumstances of life, I must *know* that I can rest on the solid fact: *God loves me!*

During a vacation in Illinois, my Florida uncle had a stroke. For days that moved into weeks, he was on the hospital's critical list. For Aunt Pearl and the family, all was uncertain, emotionally draining, and faith-stretching. There were days of progress, days of regress. In the midst of her confusion and sense of loss, I remember her repeating aloud with real conviction, "One thing I know: God loves us, and we love Him, too."

The family was finally able to take Uncle Roy home to Florida where Aunt Pearl cared for him, a helpless invalid, for five years. Much of the time he was unresponsive. She sat with him, rolled him over, bathed him, and faithfully and lovingly did all she could to make him comfortable and to communicate her love. When he died, I heard her say, "I miss him so much, even though he hasn't responded to my love for five years. But I know it's best. God is too loving to be unkind, and He is too wise to make any mistakes."

These were her simple but powerful declarations of faith and acceptance, her way of declaring God's loving care was enough—He had not forsaken her.

Let's be absolutely certain about God's relentless love for us! I know we often feel weak and failing. We may be so disgusted with ourselves that we are sure God also must feel disgusted with us. Is that the way of loving parents? No. And it is not the way of love in God. Instead of disgust, His love tenderly reaches out to the weak, to the failing, as a mother gives special, tender love to a sick or sad child.

Unfailing Goodness

If I were to ask, "Do you believe God is good?" no doubt most would quickly answer, "Yes, of course!" If I probed a bit deeper, "Do you believe that He is *always* good?" you might stop and think a bit before answering with some hesitation, "Y-e-s."

What if I got very personal with, "Do you believe that He is always good *to you*?" If you are really honest and ready to face some of your "gut" feelings, you might admit, "Well . . . not always." It's only human to have such thoughts, especially in the face of confusing reality. And it's a good idea occasionally to drag out in the full light of the Holy Spirit our secret thoughts, doubts, or questions about the Lord—His goodness, His love. As we face them honestly, they can help us move toward our goal of aligning our inaccurate thoughts about Him with truth and choose the faith way—believing against the contrary feelings. Our wrong thoughts of Him, if left unchecked, tend to widen and deepen until the gap is too wide to see His true character.

Psalm 73:1 says, "Truly (only) good is God to Israel" (AMP). That is, God is nothing other than good. He is never bad, nor does He do bad things. What does *good* mean? Certainly it is the opposite of being bad. If God were unkind, or indifferent to or neglectful of my needs, He would not be good.

To be good is to continually live up to the highest and best that we know. Since God is omniscient, He always knows what is best. Since He *is* good, without fail He lives up to the highest and best there is. Oh, to bask in the wonder of the goodness of God!

The Word of God indisputably affirms God is good:

"You are good, and do good" (Psalm 119:68).

"Rejoice the soul of Your servant, . . . For You, Lord, are good, and ready to forgive, and abundant in mercy to those who call upon You" (Psalm 86:4, 5).

"The LORD is good, a stronghold in the day of trouble; and He knows those who trust in Him" (Nahum 1:7).

A. W. Tozer says, "The goodness of God is that which disposes Him to be kind, cordial, benevolent, and full of good will toward men. He is tenderhearted and of quick sympathy. . . . By His nature He is inclined to bestow blessedness and He takes holy pleasure in the happiness of His people. . . . It is the foundation stone for all sound thought about God and is necessary for moral sanity. . . . The goodness of God is the drive behind all the blessings He daily bestows upon us."[4]

Do We Really Believe He Is Good?

In order to check how deeply we believe in God's goodness and lovingkindness, we can ask ourselves: If I really believe God loves and cares for me . . .

Why do I grumble or become discontent over the circumstances God allows to come to me?

Why am I distrustful or anxious about the future?

Why do I not thank Him more for tokens of His goodness?

How many times have I been prone to question God's goodness in the face of pain and misery?

My understanding of the goodness of God has been helped by remembering two aspects of His goodness. One is the *revealed goodness of God* which is the fact of His goodness declared in His Word. And He has given us multitudes of examples of the outworking of His goodness in the experiences of life—our own and the lives of Bible characters. For these revealed goodnesses I praise Him.

The other is the *mysterious goodness of God* when I can't see His face or understand what He is doing. I may not even be able to trace His hand in these experiences, yet I can trust Him, waiting for His explanations, thoughtfully basking in who He is, praising Him for His character, His name. "Thou art good and doest good." This is where we have to walk by faith, believing the Word of God is true when it says that God is good and does good, that He is all-powerful, even though we may not be able to put it together in our finite minds with such limited understanding.

The promise of Romans 8:28 does not mean we will

always understand everything God is doing or see the good that can come from it. Sometimes He trusts us to be unoffended with the unexplained.

Making It Personal

1. Flip back through this chapter, and discover and enlarge on each of the following:

Where does God's love originate?
What are some of the qualities of God's love?

2. One possible reason we might not recognize God's love is that there is a blockage, a hindrance. Would you be willing to pray the prayer in Psalm 139:23, 24? Ask the Holy Spirit to help you check it out as you read Isaiah 59:1, 2; Micah 3:4; and Amos 3:3.

3. What are some things a loving parent does for his or her child to show love when the child is feeling disappointed, rejected, confused? When he or she doesn't understand or has failed? The Bible says we can compare God's love for His children to a loving parent's love, except His love is much more (Matthew 5:7-11).

4. Take the comfort of God's love for you by receiving to yourself the truths in these verses. To do this, first describe His love, then write a sentence expressing your faith in His love for *you*: Romans 5:8, Ephesians 2:4-7, 1 John 4:10, Romans 8:31-39, Hebrews 12:6.

5. Check out some of the revealed goodness of God in these verses by writing the facts about His goodness stated there. How do we benefit from His goodness? (In some versions, "goodness" is translated "loving-kindness.")

Psalm 25:8, 9; 33:5
Matthew 6:30
Acts 14:17

6. In your own words, describe God's goodness. (Page 116 may help.)

7. Think of a time when you were depressed, discouraged, or anxious. Can you relate that to a questioning and doubting of God's goodness at that time?

8. Recall instances of God's goodness in your own life as a child/youth.

9. Are there some mysterious goodnesses of God affecting your life now? (See page 117.) Write a sentence or two to God declaring your trust, even though you may not be able to make sense out of it in your present circumstances.

10. From the verses we have given here, or others that you know, choose your own special verses which declare God's love and God's goodness to you. Write them on a card and carry them with you to review at free moments.

How in the
World
Should I Live?

We have to learn to interpret the mysteries of life in the light of our knowledge of God. Unless we can look the darkest, blackest fact full in the face without damaging God's character, we do not yet know Him.

Oswald Chambers,
My Utmost for His Highest

CHAPTER TEN

Unoffeneded with the Unexplained

In 1981 Rabbi Harold Kushner wrote *When Bad Things Happen to Good People*. In it he asked, "Where is this good God when bad things happen?" This question has been asked through the centuries by Christians and non-Christians. In essence it's asking, "Why is there so much pain and suffering in the world?"

Where was this good God when this bad thing happened? Did this take Him by surprise?

And why does a good God, if indeed He is good, allow, if indeed He is in control, bad things to happen to good people?

As we try to reconcile this in our minds, it seems that either He doesn't have the power to change things, or He doesn't care—He's not good. Human reason says He can't be both good and powerful. We get offended by the pain in this life when we misunderstand what God has promised when He says He is the Blessed (good) Controller (powerful).

One way of better understanding God's blessed control is to see what it's *not*. Although we have mentioned some of these facts, I believe it will help to summarize them here.

First, it doesn't mean God causes everything to happen. This would give us free reign to blame God for all the tragedies and problems in our own lives and in the world—rapes, incest, muggings, fatal accidents, divorce, family violence. No, God does not cause everything that happens.

God doesn't plan or permit a tragic occurrence *so that* He can then "bring good out of it." This is not God's way. To say that "God does bring blessings even out of bad situations . . . is quite different from saying that God *causes*, plans, or even permits tragic happenings *because* of the good that can come out of them. We know God is sovereign, but we also know that, in His sovereignty, God has placed us in a world of sin and suffering from which we have no immunity."[1]

Neither does God's blessed control mean that all events in the world and in my life are *good*. The fact that millions of Africans are starving is not good. A crippling or terminal disease is not pleasant. A broken marriage is not a blessed thing. But, as we mentioned earlier, as these things touch my life as a committed Christian, I must acknowledge God is in control and will give me grace to receive the pain, not from the hand of man, but from His own loving hand.

Neither does God's blessed control mean that God allows only good things to happen to His people. No, Christians obviously share in the pain and sorrow and death that is part of our world system. Bombs in wartime drop on God's redeemed children as well as on the unsaved. Christians suffer in accidents, from disease, from rejection, from painful relationships.

Even missionaries are part of the world system and aren't immune to bad things happening. To cite only one example, in 1987 sixteen missionaries were brutally axed to death after being bound with barbed wire by an outlaw band of anti-government rebels in Zimbabwe. No, Christians have no exemption, but we have a Person to turn to who gives a power to cope and a purpose to believe in that the unbeliever knows nothing of . . . and often, though not always, protection from evil.

God's blessed control is not blind fatalism: "What will happen, will happen." No, the very word *blessed* implies that the God who controls is a praiseworthy One. He is the same One who loves us with an everlasting love, who counts and cares for the very hairs of our head, who is moving towards the fulfillment of His marvelous plan for our lives. He is the God whose own Son hung dying on a cross. He is not a God far off, but rather near and deeply involved in the big and little events of our lives.

Trusting Him in the Unexplained

God's blessed control doesn't mean we will always understand everything God is doing. How can we explain the sudden death of a young man, committed to the Lord and to the proclamation of the gospel as a medical missionary? All our mental gyrations will never answer the why of that split-second misjudgment which sent the car careening off that mountain road.

Sometimes God trusts us to be unoffended with the unexplained, as He did with John the Baptist. In his long hours in prison, I can imagine John's thoughts could have run something like, *If Jesus really is the promised Messiah, why does He wait so long to declare Himself? Why does He leave me here in this dark, damp cell? Why hasn't He made any effort to free me? He has not even sent me a word of comfort!*

Instead of answering directly any of John's questions, all Jesus did was give him some material on which John's faith could feed. "This, John, is what's happening: 'The blind see and the lame walk; the lepers are cleansed and the deaf hear; the dead are raised up and the poor have the gospel preached to them.' " In effect, He was saying to John's messengers, "Tell John what I am doing. He's right. I do have all power. I may not be delivering him in the way he expected, but tell him to *trust me now with the unexplained.* 'Blessed is he who is not offended because of me.' "[2]

I believe John the Baptist and William Cowper would have had a lot to talk about if they had lived in the same era. I can imagine them singing together Cowper's now-famous hymn:

> God moves in a mysterious way
> His wonders to perform;
> He plants His footsteps in the sea,
> And rides upon the storm.

> Blind unbelief is sure to err,
> And scan His work in vain:
> God is His own interpreter,
> And He will make it plain.[3]

We will never fully understand God's ways or be able to give precise reasons for all His acts. He has stated this clearly.

"For My thoughts are not your thoughts, nor are your ways My ways," says the LORD. "For as the heavens are higher than the earth, so are My ways higher than your ways, and My thoughts than your thoughts" (Isaiah 55:8, 9).

But we can *know* by a faith-decision on the basis of His all-wise character that His ways and thoughts are perfect . . . no matter how bad things look or how we feel about events or people.

Wrestling with the Unexplained

Often when we are deeply shaken, a flood of questions confronts us. "Why did God let this . . . ? Why didn't He change . . . ? Why do I have to go through . . . ?" They are hard questions. Sometimes unanswerable. For a Christian who is going through a trial, yet he or she believes that our God is all-powerful and that He loves us devotedly, it's difficult to put the two together, and the person wonders, "Why is He doing this? Why is He like this?"

"There would be no sense in asking why if one did not believe in anything," Elisabeth Elliot writes. "The word itself presupposes purpose. Purpose presupposes a purposeful intelligence. Somebody has to have been responsible. It is because we believe in God that we address questions to Him. We believe that He is just and that He is love, but that belief is put to severe strain as we wrestle with our pains and perplexities, with our very position in His ordered universe."[4]

Some people say it's a bad thing to ask God why, to question what He is doing. Actually, the question itself can be either good or bad. If it is asked with an open hand, in sincere faith, with an honest desire to cooperate with the Lord in accomplishing His good purposes in my life, to learn all that I can from the situation and to grow in grace through it, then it is valuable and helpful.

But, as we touched on earlier, if it is asked with a closed fist held up toward God in a spirit of rebellion, resistance, accusation, or unbelief, then it's destructive.

God delights to have His children ask Him their honest questions—even the one who, in the midst of pain, asks in doubt. He will not deal with that one impatiently or harshly, but lovingly, longing for him or her to come again to the place of trusting. He knows our frame and remembers we are dust.[5]

"I have been with sick Christian people who torment themselves with the question, 'What is God trying to teach me?' " writes Philip Yancey. "Maybe they have it all wrong. Maybe God isn't trying to tell us anything specific each time we hurt. Pain and suffering are part and parcel of our planet, and Christians are not exempt. . . . As I look at the Bible, the evidence seems inconclusive. Sometimes God caused suffering for a specific reason—usually a warning. Sometimes Satan caused it. In other cases . . . God wasn't intending any specific message.

"Is God trying to tell us something? . . . it may be dangerous and perhaps even unscriptural to torture ourselves by looking for His message. The message may simply be that we live in a world with fixed laws, like everyone else. But from the larger view, from the view of all history, yes, God is speaking to us through pain—or perhaps, in spite of pain. He can use it to make us aware of Him. The symphony He is working out includes minor chords, dissonance, and tiring fugal passages. But those of us who follow His conducting through these early movements will, with renewed strength, someday burst into song."[6]

Did God Owe Job an Explanation?

Job, you recall, met the onset of his troubles with a strong faith response: "The LORD gave, and the LORD has taken away; blessed be the name of the LORD" (Job 1:21).

But as time went on and his "friends" taunted, questioned, and accused him, confusion came creeping in: "Even today my complaint is bitter; my hand is listless because of my groaning. Oh, that I knew where I might find Him, . . . Look, I go forward, but He is not there, and backward, but I cannot perceive Him; when He works on the left hand, I cannot behold Him; when He turns to the right hand, I cannot see Him" (23:2, 3, 8, 9).

Didn't God owe Job an explanation as to why life had been so unfair? Instead of answering Job's specific questions, out of the whirlwind God poured out a flood of questions for Job to consider.

"Where were you when I laid the foundations of the earth? Tell me, if you know so much" (38:4, TLB).

"Who decreed the boundaries of the seas when they gushed from the depths? Who . . . said, 'Thus far and no farther shall you come, and here shall your proud waves stop!'?" (38:8, 11, TLB).

"Can you ensure the proper sequence of the seasons, or . . . make lightning appear and cause it to strike as you direct it?" (38:32, 35, TLB).

"Have you given the horse strength?" (39:19, TLB).

"Is it at your command that the eagle rises high upon the cliffs to make her nest?" (39:27, TLB).

"Job, can you do any of this? I am the God who can do all of this. It's not so much answers to your questions that you need, but a fresh new look at what I am like." And Job makes a new response of faith. He chooses to let God be God as he confesses, "I know that you can do anything and that no one can stop you. You ask who it is who has so foolishly denied your providence. It is I. I was talking about things I knew nothing about and did not understand, things far too wonderful for me. . . . I had heard about you before, but now I have seen you, and I loathe myself and repent in dust and ashes" (42:2, 3, 5, 6, TLB).

God caused Job to realize something of His incomparable greatness in creation, and Job admitted there were things he would never understand. God didn't answer Job's questions; He revealed more of Himself.

Jesus Didn't Always Answer the Whys

There were times when Jesus explained mysteries and answered questions for the disciples, but there were other times when He gave no explanation. When Peter questioned Jesus' washing his feet, Jesus' answer was, "What I am doing you do not understand now, but you will know after this." And when Peter wanted to know what was going to happen to John, Jesus did not explain, but rather reminded Peter his responsibility was simply to follow Him.[7]

We could cite question after question that come to our minds. Why did a pastor in the prime of his life, with a young family and a vital ministry depending on him, suddenly collapse with a heart attack while an elderly woman lies day after day needing continual nursing care, not able to communicate with loved ones, no longer a companion to her husband? Why does the pastor die and the elderly woman live? The unexplained.

We all have times when we are overwhelmed with what seems to us a mystery of God's providence.

You may never know why your child was born with physical and mental problems.

Or why your wife or husband died when your children were still toddlers.

Or why you remain single so long when you've prayed so faithfully for a partner.

Or why God didn't answer your prayer and keep the divorce from happening.

God may be trusting you with the unexplained. The important thing is to receive the person or circumstance with that heart response of, "Yes, Lord, you are the Blessed Controller. I may not be able to understand why this has happened, but I can trust your heart of love."

No, God didn't promise an explanation for every trial. He gives us something better—the assurance that He will be with us and bring us *through* the trials as we trust Him and commit ourselves to Him.

" 'When you pass *through* the waters, I will be with you; and *through* the rivers, they shall not overflow you. When you walk *through* the fire, you shall not be burned, nor shall the flame scorch you. For I am the LORD your God, the Holy One of Israel, your Savior. . . . Fear not, for I am with you' " (Isaiah 43:2, 3, 5, italics added).

Trusting God in the Dark

I wept as I read this letter.

"For the past nine years my husband has had Alzheimer's disease. I was forty-one when this was first recognizable. He was fifty. Our two daughters were teenagers and experienced rebellion and insecurity. During the same time I was going through menopause. Through it all it has been a real life-saver for me to have had the foundation that God controls all things.

"God has seen us through the extreme struggles. Someone once told me Alzheimer's is an awful disease and I have found it to be oh so true!

1. Your friends diminish one by one.

2. You are legally and spiritually married but physically divorced.

3. Your income is lessened dramatically.

4. You gradually absorb nearly all responsibility for your family and you become a working robot.

5. Your role in the home is changed from spouse to caretaker and parent of one once your sweetheart.

6. Your home and car start crumbling little by little because there isn't time or money for upkeep.

7. You watch your mate crumble, mentally, physically little by little. You even smell the deterioration of the brain from time to time.

8. All future is wiped out except to know that your spouse will get worse and your own health will crumble."

Up to this point, dear Melanie has seen no answers to her whys. She has been called to trust God in the dark. "Who among you fears the LORD? Who obeys the voice of His Servant? Who walks in darkness and has no light? Let him trust in the name of the LORD and rely upon his God" (Isaiah 50:10).

"There are times, says Jesus, when God cannot lift the darkness from you, but trust Him. God will appear like an unkind friend, but He is not; He will appear like an unnatural Father, but He is not; He will appear like an unjust judge, but He is not. Keep the notion of the mind of God behind all things strong and growing. Nothing happens in any particular unless God's will is behind it, therefore you can rest in perfect confidence in Him."[8]

God promises blessedness to those who do not stumble at life's mysteries, who can say, "The Lord is good, therefore all that He does must be good, no matter how it looks, and I can wait for His explanations." It isn't that we won't have more questions. God understands our questionings, but if our questions keep us from trusting His goodness and wisdom, then we have forfeited His promised blessedness and peace.

Count it a real honor when God trusts you with the unexplained. During those times, the best we can do is to be still and know that He is God. To know He is in control. To declare with Job, "He knows the way that I take; when He has tested me, I shall come forth as gold."[9]

Or to affirm with the songwriter:

In heavenly love abiding,
No change my heart can fear,
And safe is such confiding,
For nothing changes here.
The storm may roar without me,
My heart may low be laid;
But God is round about me,
And can I be dismayed?[10]

There is a relief and a rest we can know as we trust Him in the dark, unoffended with the unexplained. "I may not understand, but I can trust." But does this rest and trust mean I have no other responsibility to take action? Am I just a pawn of a God who keeps me in the dark, acts arbitrarily, and pushes me around like a checker on a black-and-red board?

Making It Personal

1. Make a concise list of some of the misunderstandings we have about God's control. Does this help you better understand the pain and suffering in the world and in your world?

2. What were some of the unexplained, humanly impossible conditions Abraham faced? See Genesis 17:3-6, 15-17; 22:1, 2.

Read the New Testament commentary on this and summarize Abraham's response. See Romans 4:17-22.

3. Read Ruth 1:1-13 and describe what God had permitted to happen to Naomi. What did she conclude from what God had allowed (vv. 13, 20, 21)?

Read the rest of the book of Ruth to see how God redeemed her circumstances. Key verses: 2:8, 14-18; 4:13-17. Explain the difference in her circumstances at the end of the book.

4. Read Psalm 73. What was Asaph's first statement (v.1)? But, he had a problem. What seemingly unexplainable phenomenon was going on (vv. 2, 3)?

What specific things had he noticed about the lives of "the wicked" (vv. 4-9)?

What helped him reconcile this seeming inconsistency in God's goodness (vv. 16-20).

How does Asaph's response to God in verses 21-28 help us in our response when we are faced with frustrating, confusing, seemingly unexplainable situations?

5. Is there something in your life now that seems to have no meaning, no purpose, a mystery of God's providence, a mysterious way of God? Do you have some confused or negative thoughts about God? Based on Psalm 62:8, "Pour out your heart before Him," write out your *feeling* thoughts to God. Express yourself freely. You won't offend Him.

6. After you read these verses, can you write your *faith* thoughts to God? Will you choose, in your current circumstances, to be unoffended with the unexplained? See Isaiah 43:2-5; 50:10; 55:8, 9.

Faith is not merely a subjective state of mind. There is always a corresponding fact to which it gives substance. Nor is it merely passive. Every true act of faith is followed by an activity of faith. It grows with exercise, but atrophies through neglect.

J. Oswald Sanders,
Mighty Faith

CHAPTER ELEVEN

Am I Just a Passive Puppet?

God's blessed control doesn't negate our responsibility to take action. It doesn't give us license to hang our battle gear on a hook and languidly say, "God is in control; there's nothing I can do." Many times there *is* something we can do. If your marriage has turned sour, there are ways it can be helped, if you want help. If we've had a misunderstanding or disagreement with someone, there is something we can do—either address the problem in an attitude of love and/or extend forgiveness, if we are willing to be humbled. If we see evil rampant and increasing around us, we can speak out, if we are willing to get involved.

Actually, getting involved is the name of the game for the Body of Christ. Haven't we been given the Great Commission to "go into all the world and preach the gospel to every creature"? Didn't Jesus call us lights in a dark world? Our work in social and political concerns can bring glory to God. And we are to *work* for our daily bread. We have the promise that as we put His kingdom first, God will add to us all that we need, but He balances that with, "If anyone will not work, neither shall he eat."[1]

In none of these cases do we sit back and passively assert, "Oh, God is in control. There's nothing I can do or need to do." We meet many opportunities daily about which we *can* do something. And all the while, as we—to the best of our understanding—are living in the circle of His will, we are taking appropriate action and we are also trusting, "God is working in this. He will do what is best. He is the Blessed Controller." We have no right to use this precious truth as a crutch for laziness, lack of involvement, or lack of concern in a situation where we *can* take action.

Accepting Responsibility and Taking Risks

Queen Esther faced both sides of this truth. She could not deny all the circumstances that pointed out so clearly God was in control:

- Her people, the Jews, were in grave danger;
- Esther was chosen queen in the very court where the power lay to help the Jews;
- Cousin Mordecai was in a position where he could keep her informed.

No dispute, these were obviously God-ordained circumstances. But Esther had to make a choice: risk her life by going to the king on behalf of the Jews, or keep silent. Mordecai encouraged her to accept her high calling by reminding her that since she was a Jew, she herself would not escape the doom pronounced. If she did not accept her opportunity, God would simply raise up help from another source. His final words of wisdom were, "Who knows whether you have come to the kingdom for such a time as this?"[2]

Parents may need to be willing to take some risks in addressing issues in a loving way with their children. After much prayer, a father and mother lovingly confronted their son and his girlfriend about living together before marriage, explaining why this was unwise, that it was sin, and that they were cutting themselves off from God's rich blessings. The couple sensed the loving concern of the parents, realized their wrong, and chose to go God's way, living separately until they were married.

At one of my seminars, after I had emphasized the importance of loving confrontation, I received this letter from one in the group. "This will mark the third year since my children and I confronted their father in love and told him he must get help for his alcoholism or we would move to another home and return only when he decided to get help.

"This was one of the hardest things I have ever been asked to do. First I had to know if I was doing what the Lord wanted me to do. After spending one year educating myself on alcoholism, counseling with both Christians and non-Christians in the field, and praying to be guided clearly on each step, I knew what had to be done.

"When he said he wasn't going to get help, we moved into a small apartment and continued to pray he would change his mind. It was four long months before he did. Now my husband hasn't had a drink for three years. We as a family give many thanks for a loving God and a husband and father who was willing to get help."

Confrontation requires risk. The end result may not even be as positive as the examples given here. In any case, there are times when we must confront another. But it needs to be done with much prayer and perhaps the counsel of others.

In other less critical issues, it may also be profitable to address the need. "My husband is a physician, often comes home late, and really enjoys being alone. It seemed he never had time to listen to me or hear the concerns I have for raising our two sons. One night as we were getting ready for bed, I asked him how long he allotted his patients for an office visit. 'Fifteen minutes,' he said. 'And how much do you charge them?' 'Thirty dollars.' I went to the closet, took out my purse, and quietly and calmly handed him thirty dollars, asking for fifteen minutes of his undivided attention. I talked, he listened. Then with a twinkle he advised, 'You need to send your husband in. He really needs to listen to you more.' Now, months later, he not only asks me to share with him my concerns but seems to know when I need to talk with him and even suggests it first."

I'm Responsible for My Mind

It's also my responsibility to fill my mind and heart with God's Word, especially about God's character, as we spoke of in Chapters 8 and 9. If we are going to be comforted by our Blessed Controller, we have to have accurate thoughts about what He is really like. This is not a quick, overnight exchange, but a lifelong discipline, a constant process, a daily responsibility, a continual pattern of "bringing every thought into captivity to the obedience of Christ." When you become a Christian, God does not take out the old cartridge of wrong thinking and put in a new one that never requires any effort towards change on your part.³

In a sense, the reading of this book is in vain unless it motivates us to get to know and draw close to our dear Lord Jesus, our Blessed Controller. And that takes action on our part—time spent reading and assimilating the Word of God into our minds, so it will reach the heart and spill over into our living, disciplining our thoughts to develop the habit of seeing God in everything, not demanding explanations, but expressing worship and trust.

I'm Also Responsible to Pray

A common question is, "If the Lord is allowing 'whatever' to happen, why do we pray, asking Him to change a person or a circumstance?" How can we reconcile these two seemingly opposing concepts?

Our sovereign God has chosen to work in answer to the believing prayers of His children. God has included you and me in His plan to reach the world. He has ordained the ministry of prayer. James understood the desire of God for His children to ask when he wrote to the scattered Jewish Christians, "You do not have because you do not ask" (James 4:2). If He did not want us to ask, why would he make such promises as, "Whatever you ask in My name, that I will do, that the Father may be glorified in the Son. If you ask anything in My name, I will do it" (John 14:13, 14)?

This truth is vividly reinforced by R. Arthur Mathews in *Born for Battle*. "The Soldier of the Cross [Jesus] had taught His disciples the need to pray, 'Thy will be done on earth as it is in heaven.' The obvious inference is that God has limited certain of His activities to responding to the prayers of His people. Unless they pray, He will not act. Heaven may will something to happen, but heaven waits and encourages earth's initiative to desire that will, and then to will and pray that it happens. The will of God is not done on earth by an inexorable, juggernaut omnipotence out there overriding or ignoring the will of man on earth. On the contrary, God has willed that His hand be held back while He seeks for a man, an intercessor to plead, 'Thy will be done on earth,' in this or that specific situation."[4]

Moses was one of those intercessors. God had pronounced the exact judgment that would follow if His people Israel turned their backs on Him. Moses saw their golden calf and their constant rebellion against Him from the day they left Egypt. So . . . Moses found a cave in a rock there on Mt. Sinai, went alone into the darkness, sat down on the nearest rock, put his chin on his hands and muttered, "It's no use. What will happen, will happen. We must now wait here to be destroyed." Is that what Moses said? No, don't try to fit it into your bedtime story tonight. It isn't there. Instead, he spent the next forty days and forty nights without food and water, pleading with the Lord to save His people.[5]

Yes, Moses was one of those intercessors God is looking for. And Moses himself tells how God answered: "The Lord listened to me."[6] God did not destroy His people in this case. Obviously His will and plan for them included more years and more experiences. Using Rev. Mathews's words, heaven heeded the plea of Moses, the intercessor, in that specific situation.

Prayer is essential to fight spiritual warfare. There is a battle raging in the heavenlies. Ephesians 6 charges us to put on the armor and *pray*! God is the One who tears down Satan's strongholds and defeats the enemy, but prayer is a vital part of the victories won.

Prayer Coupled with Acceptance

On the other hand, when Paul prayed that the Lord would remove his "thorn in the flesh," God's answer was to give him grace for his weakness, and Paul was content with God's will.[7]

Jesus prayed three times that the cup of His suffering might be taken away, but each time He added, "Nevertheless, not as I will, but as You will." He was willing to accept what God was allowing, but that did not keep Him from praying for deliverance. With both Jesus and Paul, it seems there was a point at which they stopped praying for relief and simply rested in the will of God.[8]

There are certainly references in Scripture which speak of praying for restored health and relief from trials. Still, the emphasis seems to be more on asking for and receiving the marvelous grace and strength of God to endure, persevere, and glorify Him *in the midst* of difficulties and troubles.[9]

"Not that I speak in regard to need, for I have learned in whatever state I am, to be content: I know how to be abased, and I know how to abound. Everywhere and in all things I have learned both to be full and to be hungry, both to abound and to suffer need. I can do all things through Christ who strengthens me" (Philippians 4:11-13).

Paul's prayers which he wrote to various churches concentrated on holy character rather than relief from undesirable circumstances or people. "Always laboring fervently for you in prayers, that you may stand perfect and complete in all the will of God."[10]

Praying and Doing

Elisabeth Elliot tells an experience which I feel can help us find the balance between God's part and our part. She describes three areas of concern: a close friend with cancer who was enduring great pain; a well-loved

New Testament, used many years, now lost; a manuscript on which she had worked many years does not now seem publishable.

"What shall I do?" she asks. "I have done the obvious things. Prayer is the first thing—asking God to do what I *can't* do. The second thing is to get busy and do what I *can* do. I prayed for my friend, of course, and then I sat down and wrote her a letter. I don't know what else to do for her now. My husband and I prayed together about the lost New Testament (and many of my friends prayed too). We went to the proper authorities at the airline and have been assured that everything will be done to recover it, but it has not turned up. We prayed about the bad manuscript and asked for editorial advice. It looks quite irremediable. I continue to pray repeatedly, extensively, and earnestly about all of the above. And one more thing: I seek the lessons God wants to teach me, and that means that I ask why."[11]

As with any truth, resting in the wonderful fact of God's blessed control needs to be kept in balance. We are not doormats. Instead, we have the awesome privilege of partnership with the living God.

We Can't Make It Alone

Before I close this chapter, I want to emphasize that we cannot keep this balance by ourselves, we can't take action in the power of our own strength, we can't make it alone. We need the Holy Spirit's help. Stephen is a model for how we can take responsible action while being dependent on the Holy Spirit.

When Stephen, a "man full of faith and the Holy Spirit" (Acts 6:5), was performing spectacular miracles among the people, some men started an argument with him, but none of them could stand against the wisdom and the Spirit with which he was speaking. So these men secretly induced other men to lie about him: "We have heard him speak blasphemous words against Moses and God" (6:11). This so roused the crowd that they seized Stephen, dragged him away, and brought him before the council, where they repeated and enlarged upon their lies.

When the high priest asked Stephen, "Are these accusations true?", this was his opportunity to speak, and he gave a long, clear, objective, and non-vindictive defense. Stephen was no passive puppet! In the face of this ridicule, with his enemies sitting all around him and his life in danger, he told of their forefathers who persecuted and killed the prophets. Then he turned to his persecutors and said, "You stiff-necked and uncircumcised in heart and ears! You always resist the Holy Spirit; as your fathers did, so do you" (7:51).

When the Jews heard this, they were infuriated and began gnashing their teeth at him. "But he, being full of the Holy Spirit, gazed into heaven and saw the glory of God, and Jesus standing at the right hand of God" (7:55). And he told them what he was seeing! This only increased their fury, and they covered their ears, rushed at him, and, dragging him out of the city, they began to stone him.

"And they stoned Stephen as he was calling on God and saying, 'Lord Jesus, receive my spirit!' Then he knelt down and cried out with a loud voice, 'Lord, do not charge them with this sin.' " (7:59, 60). And Stephen died.

Stephen Made God His First Reference

What was Stephen's response to the ridicule, the lies, the mistreatment, the false accusations, the humiliation, the stoning? Did he demand more respectful treatment? Did he gnash back at them? Did he become vindictive? Did he point out that they were lying? None of these! "He . . . gazed into heaven," making God his first reference. As he directed his thoughts toward God and heaven, he "saw the glory of God, and Jesus standing at the right hand of God." He must have been reminded that God was in control. God was bigger than his enemies. God would be glorified in this. God was not making a mistake. This horrible event was not out of His control.

With such an awareness of the presence and the character of God, he had peace in the midst of the stoning. Stephen's heart's desire was, "Not my will, but Yours be done." He had chosen to live within the circle of God's will, therefore he could have peace in the midst of the adversity and say, "Lord Jesus, receive my spirit." Because his eyes were fixed on the Blessed Controller, he had such freedom from a vindictive and resentful spirit that he could fall on his knees, and cry out with a loud voice in the presence of them all, "Lord, do not charge them with this sin" (7:60). He had full acceptance of the circumstance that God allowed to come to him (even though it came to him from evil men with evil intentions), and he exercised the grace of forgiveness toward those who lied about and grossly mistreated him.

Stephen modeled how to put into practice the principles we've been talking about. He epitomized the godly reaction in the face of extreme adversity. *How was it possible for Stephen to respond with such a noble spirit*, such an acceptance of the situation, that he had peace within his heart and forgiveness toward his abusers and accusers? Acts 6:5 tells his secret: he was a man *full of the Holy Spirit*.

Stephen was *filled with the Spirit* and he *walked in the power of the Spirit*. This had become a way of life for him. And that is our only hope too. We can't make it on our own.

It is the Spirit who will enable us to see God in everything. It is the Spirit who will help us to yield afresh our will to His will. It is the Spirit who will help us to believe in God's blessed control and who will enable us to hand our anxiety, our trouble over to Him. It is the Spirit who gives us ability to rest enfolded in His everlasting arms, confident in His unfailing love, His indisputable goodness, His unerring wisdom, and His unlimited power. ✕

But How Can I Be Filled?

So, you say, Stephen was filled with the Spirit. How does that happen? Is it possible for me, or was Stephen in a different class, a unique person?

As believers who have received Jesus Christ as our Savior from sin, we already have the Holy Spirit dwelling within.[12] What then does it mean to "be filled with the Spirit"?

If we are going to know the fullness of the Holy Spirit in the varied conditions of our lives, we must *abandon ourselves to Him*. Stephen Olford expresses it this way. "Yes, He [the Holy Spirit] *did* come in at conversion. He's dormant there, but is He dominant? He's present there, but is He president? You possess Him, but does He possess you?"[13]

Relating this to our diagram, we could ask, "Are you living within the circle of God's *will*? Are you committed to going His way, to cooperating with Him? Are you continually making that choice to seek His will and way, not your own?" If we are allowing no known sin, and if we have made this basic commitment to the will of God, the Holy Spirit will eagerly respond to us with His presence, His power, and His loving control of our whole being. *Let's daily ask Him to fill us afresh for today's needs*. And purpose to walk in the power of the Spirit throughout the day.

James H. McConkey explained it, "When we surrender our *sins* and believe, we *receive* the Holy Spirit.

When we surrender our *lives* and believe, we are *filled* with the Holy Spirit. . . . At conversion the Spirit enters. At surrender the Spirit, already entered, takes full possession."[14]

✳ As I was reading of Stephen and his gracious response, my heart welled up in prayer, "Blessed Lord, I am yours. So fill me now with your Spirit that in the midst of even extreme trouble, by the gracious power of your loving Spirit, my divine Helper, I will gaze intently into heaven and see You and Jesus standing at Your right hand, seeing you in everything that touches me. So fill me afresh, dear Lord, with the Holy Spirit that I will have this response in the midst of a small or large crisis today. May I learn in the little choices of life to walk in the Spirit, making you my first reference, for I know that this is the path to peace when the big troubles come too."

God is bigger than any person or happening that touches our lives. When we acknowledge His control, we are not saying He merely uses us as puppets and pulls a few strings to manipulate us. God has given us a free will which is an actual freedom to choose. And He has provided the indwelling Holy Spirit who, as we yield ourselves to Him and draw upon His strength, enables us to take responsible steps of action and respond with gratitude. ✳

Making It Personal

1. The Christian life is a life of faith. We are constantly told to believe, rest, trust. Our new life springs from God, not from anything in us (Ephesians 2:8-10).

It is God who_____. 1 John 1:9
It is God who_____. Romans 3:24, 5:1
It is God who_____. 2 Corinthians 5:21
It is God who_____. Ephesians 1:3

2. We are also given some clear directives as to things *we are to do*. Describe those you find in these verses:

Romans 10:9, 10
1 Peter 5:8, 9; James 4:7
John 16:23, 24; 1 John 5:14, 15
Ephesians 6:11-17
2 Timothy 2:15; Acts 17:11; Psalm 119:11, 18, 38

3. Describe other steps of action Christians can take to be a light in a dark world. Is there some action you can take this week in the power of the Holy Spirit to let your light shine?

4. How has God planned that our prayers fit in with His sovereign plans? (Refer to page 139.)

5. Describe a current problem for which you need wisdom, direction. What part of it is totally out of *your* control? Is there anything about it you *can* change? (Sometimes the only action we can take is to pray and to choose a new response of commitment and trust.)

6. Briefly state any evidences you see that Stephen was depending on the Holy Spirit *while* he was taking responsible action. (See Acts 6 and 7.)

7. From these verses, discover why we need the Holy Spirit. We can't make it alone!

John 14:26
Romans 8:14-17
Romans 8:26-27
1 Corinthians 12:4-11
Galatians 5:16, 22, 23

8. Copy from this chapter James McConkey's one-sentence explanation of *how* we are filled with the Holy Spirit. We may need to take this action many times a day, especially at the beginning of our walk in the Spirit. Make this a habit of your life this week.

*Seek to cultivate a buoyant, joyous sense of the
crowded kindnesses of God in your daily life.*

Alexander Maclaren,
Joy with Strength

*Then let thy life through all its ways
One long thanksgiving be,
Its theme of joy, its song of praise,
"Christ died, and rose for me."*

J. B. S. Monsell,
Joy and Strength

CHAPTER TWELVE

Attitude:
Gratitude

The phone rang. It was Nettie from the office. Some
potential buyers were coming to look at our building.
She knew I'd want to be praying as they compared the
building to their needs.

Yes, this was good news! I was glad to know that
there were some serious lookers. Four years ago, we had
put our office building up for sale. Again and again during those years of waiting, interested parties would

appear, our hopes would rise, their interest would wane, the deal would fall through.

Now, however, as the days went on, this looked like a sure sell. The contract was carefully prepared and verbally approved. All we needed were the proper signatures, and this was scheduled for the following Monday. What a relief! Now we could get on with our plans for relocation into a facility that would better meet our current needs.

We waited expectantly through the day on Monday. Nothing happened. I resisted the urge to call our realtor. Finally, late Tuesday, he called and said the company decided *not* to buy our building.

My first reference was to God, but with more groaning than acceptance. "Father, I thought sure it was going to sell this time. Don't you want us to get on with life? Isn't our ministry to people more important that caring for administrative details? Where are you in this, Father? It almost seems you don't care."

Then He seemed to tenderly draw me back with, "Yes, I understand your questions. But don't forget I *am* interested in what is best for you. I am *presently* working for your good. I did allow this to happen, but I am still in control."

With the backdrop of this awareness, our conversation continued, "Thank you, Lord—you do care about us. You know all about this. You allowed this deal to fall through. Thank you that you are in control. Thank you that you are presently working for our best. I choose to trust you for the right timing in selling this building."

Give Thanks in All Circumstances

An attitude of gratitude is a major ingredient in letting the truth of God's blessed control work out into the dailies of life. The clear and challenging command from

1 Thessalonians 5:18 is, "Give thanks *in all circumstances,* for this is God's will for you in Christ Jesus."[1] There are very few times in Scripture when God spells out His will so specifically. Perhaps He knew this would be a hard one for us.

I remember the first time this came home to me. I was in grad school. This very excellent Christian college had some pretty clear rules which were intended to encourage all the students toward high standards of Christian conduct. One rule was that men and women students could not ride in the same car overnight without special faculty permission. This, of course, especially applied to travel during vacation times when many of us would leave after classes and drive all night to get home as soon as possible. It seemed like a good rule to me.

When it was time to seriously plan for Christmas vacation, I didn't have to wonder how I would travel those twenty-four hours. A couple from my home town invited me to ride with them and their two children. This seemed like a wise and practical plan. Then I remembered the rule.

When I asked the dean of women if that applied to my riding home with this family, she said, "Yes, you will need to write a letter to the faculty requesting permission." I rather thought she could have added, "This is routine, and I'm sure in this case permission will be granted," but she didn't give me a clue! To me, the whole situation seemed a bit extreme, but I deeply respected the godly faculty and settled down to write the letter of request.

While waiting for their decision, I began thinking. *What if they deny me the privilege? How would I ever explain to the folks at home why I didn't ride with my friends? Would they understand the rule? Would they respect my college?* I was struggling with this on the very morning I was to go in for the faculty decision.

In my Bible reading that morning I read, "In every thing give thanks: for this is the will of God in Christ Jesus concerning you" (1 Thessalonians 5:18, KJV). It stood out as though written on the wall in boldface type and giant letters. IN EVERYTHING GIVE THANKS! I knew the Lord was referring to the circumstance that I was facing that day. What would be the faculty's decision?

Then, as if the command to give thanks wasn't enough, the bold and giant letters announced, FOR THIS IS THE WILL OF GOD IN CHRIST JESUS CONCERNING YOU. Wow! How could it be any more direct or clear than that? Because I knew it was the will of God for me to be in that school, I also knew the rules of the school were the will of God for me at that moment. Now, added to that, I knew it was the will of God for me to give thanks to Him *in everything*. That included this seemingly illogical situation.

I sincerely wanted to do the will of God so I knew what I had to do in regard to the faculty verdict—even if it seemed unreasonable or nonsensical to me or to others. Whatever the response of others might be, my responsibility was to give thanks and trust God to work out all the ramifications.

With my Bible still open to the will of God for me, I lined my will up with His. "I choose to thank you, Lord, *in* this situation. I thank You for the decision of the faculty. Whatever it is, it's all right with me."

Permission was granted and all of my concern may seem wasted, but, looking back, I'm glad they had the rule. I'm glad the dean didn't explain it away as a routine permission request, because it allowed the Lord to begin working in my life the habit of giving thanks *in everything*.

Are We to Give Thanks for *All* Things?

There is one big question about this giving of thanks that arises out of Ephesians 5:20, "Giving thanks always for all things to God the Father in the name of our Lord Jesus Christ." *as this us applies to my life & me*

Some maintain that this teaches we must give thanks *for* all things that come into our lives, whatever their origin. Commenting first on the verse in Thessalonians, Michael Baughen's explanation helps us get a balanced perspective. "It is important to get this clear: '*in* all circumstances,' not '*for* all circumstances.' The idea of praising God for disasters, tragedies, and illnesses has gained currency amongst some Christians in recent years. It is put across as the way of high Christian living, of triumphant faith. But is this really what the Bible teaches? . . . But what about Ephesians 5:20, some will say? 'Always and for everything giving thanks . . .' Can this phrase 'for everything' actually mean that I should thank God for someone who is living immorally, or for my friend being killed in a highway accident, or for a person going blind, or someone being cruel to his wife? If so, I am being asked to give praise for evil and nowhere in the Scriptures is such a thing countenanced."[2]

Actually, the very opposite is true. We are told to "have nothing to do with the fruitless deeds of darkness."[3] Instead, we are to avoid them, fight them, expose them. And that is certainly not compatible with the idea of giving thanks for evil and sin!

Though we don't thank God for anything related to the fallenness of this world, we can obey the command to give thanks "in all circumstances." Even when the situation is bad or seemingly hopeless, we can always thank God for His love, His wisdom, and His care for us in all things. In this case, "thank you" becomes an expression of faith. As we previously discussed, though God may not have ordered the thing, we can thank Him that even this was filtered through His love and grace. And though the thing itself may not *be* the will of God, by the time it comes to me it becomes the *permissive* will of God for me and is to be accepted at that point as coming from His hand to me, not from any second causes. He is there to compel this event, these people, to work together for my good. We don't thank God for the misery, but we can give thanks to the Lord in the midst of it.

Too Wise to Make Any Mistakes

Giving thanks is the expression of my confident trust that God is too wise to make any mistakes and too loving to be unkind in His dealing with me. So that,

> When you have three boys and you want a girl so badly . . .

> When you are unable to have *any* children . . .

> When you've had enough of the loneliness of being single . . .

> When you are in the middle of a messy divorce . . .

> When you'd give anything to stay home with your children, but you must work to eat . . .

> When you discover your young teenager is using drugs . . .

> When the boss expects *more* overtime and you're already stressed out . . .

> When your nest is empty and now your husband has some strange physical problems . . .

you have a proper spirit of gratitude, based on the character of God. It springs from the assurance that God is who He claims to be and that "no good thing will He withhold from those who walk uprightly" (Psalm 84:11). It is a confidence that He loves us and is making no mistakes. That is real faith!

It takes some learning to habitually walk in this attitude of gratitude which is independent of circumstances, happenings, and people, but it is possible to learn the thanksgiving response—to "continually offer up a sacrifice of praise to God, that is, the fruit of lips that give thanks to His name" (Hebrews 13:15, NASB). Some of us may have more to *unlearn* than others, like those who fit into this graphic description:

"Complaining can develop into a fine art! Some tarnished souls can look at any situation and tell you what is wrong with it. Such people are 'walking minus signs.' Unfortunately, a few of these sour spirits have joined our churches. They look as though they sucked lemons for breakfast. One of these saints is said to have lived complaining and died complaining. When he finally got to Heaven, his first comment was, 'The halo doesn't fit!' "[4]

Discontent Expressed in Finding Fault

Opposite a spirit of gratitude is a spirit of complaint. Mixed with that is deep discontent which is expressed in finding fault—with our circumstances, with the God of our circumstances, with the people in our world. Sometimes we discreetly label this "discernment," when actually it is rehearsing the shortcomings of people and censuring God's ways. It's hard to call it what it really is—discontentment with the ways of God.

Time and again we find the children of Israel grumbling about what God provided for them or what He didn't provide. They grumbled about their water. They grumbled about their food. They grumbled against Moses and Aaron, their leaders. Moses called it by its real name. "Your murmurings are not against us but against the LORD."[5]

The Psalmist tells us that when the Lord heard the complainings of His people, His anger came up against them "because they did not believe in God, and did not *trust* in His salvation" (Psalm 78:22, italics added). At the bottom line, all complaining means that we are not trusting God. In contrast, an attitude of gratitude is an evidence that we are living by faith, trusting in the goodness of the Lord.

Building Monuments of Gratitude

One time after I had presented the concept, "God is the Blessed Controller of all things," someone in the audience exclaimed aloud, as though a light had just turned on, "Oh, He is in control of the *good* things that happen in our lives, too, isn't He?" Yes, He is, and we need to recognize that "every good gift and every perfect gift is from above, and comes down from the Father" (James 1:17).

Tracing the Lord's steps in our lives gives us substance for praise and thanksgiving. He is LORD! He is not only Lord of my adversity, He is Lord of my prosperity.

Thanking God in advance for His promised grace to help in time of need—that's faith. And faith in God is built on God's faithfulness in the past:

The sureness of His Word,
The solidness of His character,
The perfect fulfillment of His promises,
His unending provision for our needs.

By building a monument to God's faithfulness in our yesterdays we:

Enlarge our faith for present needs,
Prepare for the uncertainties of the future,
Build good habits in the good times so we are
  better able to give thanks when trials come.

Amy Carmichael advises us to put the truth of God's faithfulness in our storehouse of memory.

The classic example of a monument erected to God's faithfulness is the twelve-stone memorial, hand-carried from the middle of the Jordan River after the children of Israel had crossed on dry ground. Obeying God's command, they set up the stones at Gilgal to proclaim, "This, my children, is what your God did. This is what He is able to do. You can trust Him for tomorrow too."[6]

And have you noticed the many word-monuments in Scripture—clear descriptions of the past mercies of the Lord? Moses built such a monument. And Joshua. And David. The Levites of Nehemiah's time. Mary and Zacharias, Stephen and Paul.[7]

"It is well to quote past experiences as arguments for faith. Our past life will have missed its aim if it has not revealed God to us. Each incident is intended to show us some new trait in his character for us to treasure for all coming time. Not that we expect God to repeat Himself; but that we learn to say, if He did all this, He is resourceful, tender-hearted, wise and strong: there is no emergency with which He cannot grapple, no need He cannot fulfill. He gave manna—He surely can provide water. He delivered from Egypt—He can certainly emancipate from Babylon."[8]

Projects for Building Gratitude

We each have, as it were, a treasure chest full of God's faithfulness, placed there through the history of His past goodness to us. Have we opened up these treasure chests? Have we used their riches?

One way is to look for one blessing for the day, one memory of that day's goodness. This came to mind vividly as I was preparing my projector and tape player for use while speaking in Bozeman, Montana. The coffee ladies were getting ready to serve three hundred cups of coffee too, and we all needed electrical cords. As I walked off the platform and down the aisle, I congratulated myself, "Good, Verna, things are well-prepared to begin the meeting in a few minutes." It's always so good to know things are prepared, to know we can start on time and there will be no hitches in the sound, the projection, or the music. These last-minute checks had been made.

When I got to the back of the auditorium, I realized I had left my Kleenex at the front. As I turned to retrieve the little package, I saw a lady unplugging all my cords, ready to walk off with my extension cord! A coffee lady who had no idea she was taking the speaker's equipment! As we laughed and put it all back together, I put that little incident in my treasure chest and pulled it out later as God's blessing to me that day. God brought me back for my Kleenex, and I was able to avert quite a bit of confusion and delay as we met the three hundred ladies that morning.

> "It is good to give thanks to the LORD, and to
> sing praises to Your name, O Most High; . . .
> For you, LORD, have made me glad through
> Your work; I will triumph in the works of
> Your hands" (Psalm 92:1, 4).

Frances Ridley Havergal, a poet and songwriter, kept a journal of God's mercies. She was always on the lookout for indications of the Lord's grace and generosity, and she found them everywhere.

Another friend writes notes and dates in her Bible, recording specific goodnesses of the Lord to her. Her Bible is becoming to her more and more a history of her own life and experience and in itself a journal of mercies.

A family made their own plan for looking back and making monuments to God's faithfulness: "About six months ago, my husband initiated our Journal of Gratefulness to God. He had me buy a five-year diary. Once a week, for our family devotion time, we make entries of what special ways God has shown His hand toward us that past week—either specific answers to prayer or some situation that was God's obvious doing. Occasionally we look back through parts of it and are encouraged in our faith and reminded to thank God for what He has done. It also helps us to become aware of things that are important to others in the family. Each of us has enjoyed this practice, and we expect it to continue to build our faith and thankfulness for years to come."[9]

So the record, the journal of mercies, could be a memorial of yesterday to witness to children and grandchildren the faithfulness of the Lord. It can serve as an encourager or a promoter of faith to us during down times, and it can provide a platform for praise and thanksgiving.

Many a complaining life would be changed into song by a journal of mercies. Many a fear will vanish by recalling a past evidence of God's mercy. Memory can be made the precursor of hope. Yesterday's blessing can inspire courage for today. This is what the past can do for us if we will let it.

How Can We Develop an Attitude of Gratitude?

1. Realize that an ungrateful attitude expressed in grumbling is sin. Whether the grumbling is outward and verbal or more inward and quiet, grumbling is sin. Confess it as sin.

2. Choose an attitude of gratitude. Choose to put away grumbling and purpose to let thanksgiving be our pattern for living. Pray for an increasing spirit of praise and thanksgiving in our lives.

3. Think and express gratitude. Set our hearts to the exercise of praise and thanksgiving to the Lord early in our day. Praise Him for His past and present mercies. To help in this we could keep a Journal of God's Mercies.

4. Practice accepting our present circumstances with thanksgiving. Purpose to apply the "in everything give thanks" principle in our daily living. And don't forget, it's as we learn to walk in that truth day by day in the little things of life that we are being prepared for the bigger, more critical issues that will confront us.

An attitude of gratitude speaks volumes both to God and to the people around us. It says,

- I have no grudge against God for allowing this thing in my life.

- I have no bitterness toward the person who seems to be the human agent in bringing this into my life.

- I believe God is good and is doing the very best for me in this present moment.

- I believe God will be faithful to fulfill His promises to me for that future need.

Making It Personal

1. What is the attitude opposite of gratitude?

2. What was God's response to the grumblings of the children of Israel? See Numbers 14:26-35.

3. Describe the spirit of ingratitude expressed in these verses:

Luke 17:17, 18
2 Timothy 3:2
Psalm 106:7
Isaiah 1:2
2 Chronicles 32:24-26

4. Can you think of a recent situation in which you found it difficult to obey the command, "in everything give thanks"? Describe the situation. What did you choose to do?

5. What is the difference between "in everything give thanks" and giving thanks "for everything"?

6. Why are we to practice walking in the "in-every-thing-give-thanks" way? See 1 Thessalonians 5:18.

7. Make a list of people to whom you could express gratitude. What did each do for you, mean to you, give to you? Write one letter, make one phone call, or speak to one person expressing your thanks.

8. What do these verses teach us to give thanks for?

Romans 6:17, 18
2 Thessalonians 1:3
1 Timothy 1:12
Psalm 107:1, 2
John 6:11

9. Read again the four steps, "How Can We Develop an Attitude of Gratitude?" (pages 159-160). Will you commit yourself to begin taking these steps this week?

10. Plan a project (as suggested on page 157) for remembering God's past and present mercies. Talk about some of your blessings with one person each day this week.

*They [Israel in the wilderness] were no longer
satisfied with what God provided. For us this
means Jesus, and He is all God ever promised us.
He may add or take away a great many other
mercies, but all we actually need to be content is
in Jesus. . . . When we long for the things this
world can give, when we feel others have much
and we have nothing, when life seems intolerably
dull, we are, in fact, confessing that Christ has
ceased to satisfy us.*

Patricia St. John,
Missing the Mark

CHAPTER THIRTEEN

The Bottom Line

I had carried in the last box of books, the last bag of
groceries. It wouldn't take long to settle into my two-
week haven at the motel—away from the office, from
people, from telephones, from questions, from decisions.
Ah, now to put on my comfy grubbies and get on with
my purpose for being there—to begin research for a new
book. After weeks of anticipation, there I was!

Books were spread out, tape recorder set, notes at
hand, pencil poised, when the whole room began to

shake. Table, lamps, bed, refrigerator—everything. My first writings looked more like hieroglyphics than English. After a short while, the movement stopped, only to be repeated many times throughout that first day, and the next, and the next.

Although it turned out to be only a large motel washing machine that had been installed wrong, while the shaking was in progress, I couldn't function normally. Every shaking was a vivid picture to me of the uncertain world around. Just as our bodies can't function well when all around is shaking, so our souls cannot find rest while leaning on shakable things.[1]

What Are Our Basic Soul-Needs?

That led me to ponder, just what *are* the needs of our souls and where is the solid, unshaking ground? What is the bottom line? What do we *really* need? Much has been spoken and written in recent years about the basic needs of the human soul. A variety of words have been used, but a simple, comprehensive description is security and meaning.

All I really need in life for satisfaction is a sense of security, and meaning and purpose in life. *All*. It sounds so simple. Yet it becomes so complex. As Americans with parents and grandparents who experienced the Great Depression of the 1930s, we have been programmed to believe that security is owning our own home, having a job with benefits in a stable company, and a cushion of savings in the bank. Our security goes on to include a loving spouse, obedient children, and a warm, caring body of believers.

A life which is full of meaning is more personalized and therefore more elusive. Some women in the business world today may say it's being recognized as an equal with their male counterparts. The executive may say, "It's getting to the top." To one with a talent, it's "being discovered" and put on display. To the mother fulfilling her daily unsung duties, it's the longing to feel that she's worth something, that there's purpose and meaning to the diaper pail, the spilled milk, and the runny noses. And most of all, that she's loved and appreciated. We can also wrap it up in one word and call it our need for fulfillment.

Totally apart from our great American dream, we need to ask, "How does God plan for our soul-needs to be met? From whom or what do we derive our ultimate satisfaction?" Even the most newborn Christian could probably give an answer that would satisfy theologians: "Jesus Christ is all we need." Or someone will repeat a favorite promise, "My God shall supply all your need according to His riches in glory by Christ Jesus" (Philippians 4:19). We have no trouble declaring the sufficiency of Christ, but is that where we are actually looking to have our needs met?

Most of us behave as if people, events, and circumstances are the vehicles that will bring us fulfillment. When events and circumstances are pleasant and going my way, when people are responding to me lovingly and acceptingly, I draw my security and my meaning, my significance from these. What happens when people reject me, fail me, ignore me; when circumstances are not to my liking and life is turning sour?

When All Natural Sources Are Exhausted

Larry Crabb makes this radical statement: "We literally need nothing but the Lord and what He chooses to provide."[2] That, my friend, is the bottom line, the unshakable. Most of us have had very little experience drawing our security and significance directly from God Himself. We have our own personal resources—our intelligence, our social abilities, our appearance, our healthy bodies. We draw greatly on our own strengths, our material resources, and as much as we can from the love and acceptance of others. It's usually not until we have exhausted all these natural sources that we are forced to find how adequate the Lord Himself is to meet our needs.

At college, Jody met and married the man of her dreams. He proved to be more than she had dreamed a husband could be. He loved her dearly and showed his love in thoughtful ways. "In fact," she claimed, "he met every need I ever had to feel special and loved."

"Four years later, after the birth of our second child, my world caved in," she continued. "One night I awoke with an unexplainable fear. My heart raced, my body went weak all over. Growing up in a very ungodly home I had experienced all kinds of emotional pain, but that was nothing compared to this. I didn't understand how I, a Christian, could be feeling what I was feeling.

"The fear didn't go away. The fact that there was no reason for it only made it worse. For months my nights were spent in heart-racing, wild terror. My dear husband, who had so tenderly nurtured me and bound up all my hurts previously, could do absolutely nothing to reach me now. I would turn from his tender embrace, his gentle reminders of God's loving care, and run from him to walk the floor. I had convinced myself this was the only way to keep from snapping altogether. This lasted for over a year.

"All that year the only book of the Bible I could read was the Psalms. I deeply identified with David's struggles, 'My soul is in anguish. How long, O LORD, how long? . . . I am worn out from groaning; all night long I flood my bed with weeping. . . . Will you forget me forever? . . . How long must I wrestle with my thoughts and every day have sorrow in my heart?' " (Psalm 6:3, 6; 13:1, 2, NIV).

As she kept reading the Psalms she realized, "Lord, you really do allow terror and deep distress to touch your loved ones. David, a man after your own heart, experienced this same terror." Slowly, she began to see from David's example how to deal with her own fears. David didn't deny his frustration. He didn't try to hide from God. He poured it all out to the Lord, yet he ended his struggle by admitting his help was *in God alone*.

"The God I was running from was the only God who could help me," Jody concluded. "I no longer hid from Him. His Word became my life support. These verses were literally fulfilled in my life: 'He reached down from on high and took hold of me; he drew me out of deep waters. He rescued me from my powerful enemy, from my foes, who were too strong for me. . . . He brought me out into a spacious place; he rescued me because he delighted in me" (Psalm 18:16, 17, 19, NIV).

"My dear, loving husband, who *wanted* to help me out of this pit, could do nothing to rescue me. There was no deliverer but God Himself. And I had found Him to be just that."

What Part Do People Play?

But, you say, if it is true that I need nothing but the Lord and what He chooses to provide, where do people fit into my life? Are we not to love, encourage, and care for one another? Certainly the Bible makes clear our responsibility to love, show kindness, help in material needs, spend time together, etc.[3] These are part of what the Lord chooses to provide. All of them add to our sense of fulfillment. But if we are depending on human resources to meet our ultimate needs, whether they be our own or someone else's, when we get to the bottom line and our world is falling apart, we will find ourselves empty and withered.

Larry Crabb further explains, "Restricting dependency to God does not, however, minimize the importance and desirability of human relationships. It is right and normal to derive a wonderful sense of security from the love and fellowship of a spouse, friends, of brothers and sisters in Christ. When God blesses me with the love of other people, I am to respond gratefully by enjoying their love and basking in the security it brings. But I am to recognize that my deepest need for security is now being met and always will be met by an eternal, unchanging God of love. If loved ones turn on me, if I am placed in a situation where warm fellowship is unavailable, I am to aggressively believe that the biblical route to meeting security needs is to recognize that the sovereign God of the universe loves me. He is all that I need because He will arrange my world down to every minute detail (to believe that requires belief in a big God) in such a way that all my most basic needs will be met if I trust Him. Therefore, whatever happens to me, whether insults, loss of love, rejection, snubbing, not being invited to a certain social gathering, I am to respond with the rational, trusting response of thanksgiving."[4]

Finding Ultimate Satisfaction

It's easy to slip into the habit of looking for stability and heart satisfaction in all the wrong places. Sometimes we find ourselves, as the children of Israel in Jeremiah's day, endeavoring to get our thirst quenched through things we think will quench our thirst, only to find that we have "hewn cisterns that can hold no water" and "forsaken the fountain of living waters."[5]

So it is a gracious act of the Lord, springing out of His tenderest love, to turn us from our broken cisterns by shaking our self-sufficiency, our independence, our reliance on possessions, fame, name, health, children, or even on our devotions or spiritual exercises. His shaking of our circumstances is always out of love, that we might be moved to find our needs all the more met in Him, and thus find ultimate security. He alone is our stability!

It does not take many words to put before us the unshakable things. They can be reduced to:

God
His Word

The list of the shakable is more complex. Even the mere admission that these things are temporary, fleeting, brings a wave of uncertainty over our souls like a dark cloud. What if every shakable thing were taken away today—possessions, comforts, conveniences, meaningful work, social position, financial security, even family and friends? We would be reduced to the bottom line.

Mike and Linda Thomas very suddenly found themselves sitting on that line. When the Communists were taking over Ethiopia, this missionary family was robbed of all their possessions, including their car. Linda and the children were taken to Addis Ababa. Mike became a hostage. There was no tangible way they could comfort one another. Their human props were gone. Naturally, through the years of their marriage they had drawn strength from the warmth of their love for one another. But they were also both well aware that their ultimate trust had to be in that which is unshakable. Things which no Communist army could touch. And they found God to be abundantly adequate even though their world had caved in.

Are we expecting our husband, our wife, our friends, other family members to satisfy our soul-needs? Then beware. Hebrews 12:26-28 tells us that God will one day "shake" the tangible things. All that is impermanent will be removed and only the unshakable things will remain. If we are not to have the rug pulled out from under us some day, we had better find out now just what is unshakable. We must each come to the place David did when he wrote, "My soul waits in silence for *God only*; from Him is my salvation. *He only* is my rock and my salvation, my stronghold; *I shall not be greatly shaken*" (Psalm 62:1, 2, NASB, italics added).

Jesus' Secret of Satisfaction

As a man, Jesus knew how to draw His satisfaction from His Father. F. B. Meyer wrote, "The secrets of Jesus were the perpetual presence of God in His soul, and His never-faltering faith in the loving, careful providence of God in all the experiences of His chequered life. Can we not have this? We may if we are willing to pay the price.

"If we will resign or surrender our will utterly to Him;

"If we will tear down every veil that might hide His face, and throw open our whole being to His indwelling and use;

"If we will cease scheming, planning, devising, and fall back on the absolute care and arrangements of God;

"If we will learn to reckon on God as absolutely as on any resourceful human friend;

"If we will dare to believe that God holds Himself responsible for the sustenance and equipment for duty of all who absolutely see His glory."[6]

Jesus' life declared, "God is the Blessed Controller of all things." He had utterly surrendered His will to the Father. The basis for peace is absolute confidence in and loyalty to our Lord and full commitment to His will. If my purpose, my goal in life, doesn't line up with this, if it is rather to fulfill selfish ends which never satisfy, then I will tend to question the events of my life instead of seeing them as under His control. Life will be more complaint than contentment.

The apostle Paul had this attitude in his distressing circumstances. With the prospect of "bonds and afflictions" to come, he said, "But none of these things move me; nor do I count my life dear to myself, so that I may finish my race with joy, and the ministry which I received from the Lord Jesus, to testify to the gospel of the grace of God" (Acts 20:24).

Paul's purpose aligned with the purpose of God—to finish his ministry of faithfully giving out the good news of the gospel. Because his will was one with the will of God, he coulu say, "None of my circumstances are shaking me." He was resting in the Unshakable One.

Sometimes we jokingly say, "When all else fails, read the directions." With great solemnity we must say, *"Before* all else fails, draw from the source that never runs dry, the Person who planned to be the ultimate Meeter-of-Needs, God Himself."

When things go awry in the everyday circumstances of our lives, are we learning to say to ourselves, "God is the Blessed Controller of all things"?

Have we taken some steps to a new life of peace and greater usefulness in the purposes of God in this shaking world? Have we begun to practice drawing closer to Him by making Him our first reference in every situation, seeing Him in everything, calling Him the Blessed Controller, believing that the events of our lives are all Father-filtered, and trusting Him with the unexplained?

In a shaking world, we turn to the only One who can satisfy "the last aching abyss of the human heart."[7]

He is the *Blessed* Controller of all things, even when our world seems to be falling apart.

Making It Personal

1. After reading this chapter, how would you describe "the bottom line" as we are using the expression here?

2. List some of the sources from which you tend to draw your fulfillment and satisfaction. Beside that list, make a list of things that are shakable, temporary. How do the lists compare?

3. Can you think of anything related to God and His Word that would expand on your list of the unshakable? (Example: My position in Christ.)

4. Can you describe a time when life was reduced to God and you, nothing more? How did you respond?

5. Can you summarize what F. B. Meyer tells us is the price we must pay if we are to know Jesus' secret of satisfaction?

6. These verses describe what God does for those who wait *only* for Him (Psalm 62:5). What does each one say to you?

> Psalms 25:4, 5; 27:14; 37:34; 40:1, 2; 62:1; 104:27, 28
> Isaiah 40:31
> Lamentations 3:25

7. Although we cannot draw our security from people and things around us, what does Scripture tell us we should do for one another?

> Romans 12:9-18; 15:1, 2, 7
> Galatians 6:2
> Ephesians 4:2
> 1 Thessalonians 5:11-15
> Hebrews 13:1-3

8. How would you answer this: What am I doing to help one other person mature in Christ? If your answer is, "Very little," or maybe, "Nothing," will you pray that God will give you this opportunity with one person?

9. How can the following statements help us learn to draw our satisfaction and fulfillment from God only?

- God is the Blessed Controller of all things.
- See God in everything.
- Make God our first reference.
- Trust Him with the unexplained.
- See events as Father-filtered.

10. What concepts have been most helpful as you have read and studied through this book? How are your attitudes changing in response?

11. What does "God is the Blessed Controller of all things" mean to you now? Has this truth made any difference in your response to events and people in your day-to-day life?

NOTES

Chapter 1: He's Got the Whole World in His Hands

1. Mrs. F. W. Suffield, "God Is Still on the Throne" from *Songs Everybody Loves* (Grand Rapids, Mich.: Singspiration, 1929).

Chapter 2: Father Knows Best

1. The foundation of this relationship with God is receiving Jesus Christ as your Savior from sin. The Bible teaches that God is holy and cannot tolerate sin. We "all have sinned and fall short of the glory of God" (Romans 3:23). Jesus Christ made the way back to God for us by His death on the cross.

He said, "I am the way, the truth, and the life. No one comes to the Father except through Me" (John 14:6).

Christ promises those who turn to Him: "He who hears My word and believes in Him who sent Me has everlasting life, and shall not come into judgment, but has passed from death into life" (John 5:24). You can come to Him now by surrendering your heart and life to Jesus Christ. The Bible says, "As many as received Him, to them He gave the right to become children of God, to those who believe in His name" (John 1:12).

To invite Christ into your life, you can pray something like this: "Lord Jesus, I know I am a sinner. Thank You for dying on the cross to pay for my sin. I invite You now to come into my life, forgive my sin and be my Savior and the Lord of my life. Thank You for making me Your child. Amen."

2. See Psalm 32:8; 37:4, 5; Proverbs 3:5, 6.

3. See Deuteronomy 4:40; 5:29, 33; 6:3, 18; 12:25, 28.

4. Hannah Whitall Smith, *The Christian's Secret of a Happy Life* (Old Tappan, N.J.: Fleming H. Revell Company, 1952), p. 47.

5. Amy Carmichael, *Edges of His Ways* (Fort Washington, Penn.: Christian Literature Crusade, 1955), p. 79.

Chapter 3: Father's Incredible Promise

1. Jerry Jones, "When It's Hard to Trust," *Virtue*, March/April 1985, p. 42.

2. See 1 Peter 5:10.

3. Jones, p. 42. Also recommended reading: Helen Roseveare, *Living Sacrifice* (Minneapolis, Minn.: Bethany House Publishers, 1979).

Chapter 4: Is Everything Under God's Control?

1. See 2 Chronicles 20:6.

2. See Genesis 37-50.

3. See Matthew 4:1, Acts 5:3, 1 Peter 5:8, Revelation 12:9.

4. See Job 1:2, 3, 9-12.

5. See Job 1:13-19.

6. See Job 1:20.

7. See Revelation 4:8 and 1 John 4:4.

8. See Job 2:5, 6.

9. F. B. Meyer, *Great Verses Through the Bible* (Marshall, Morgan and Scott, 1966; reprint ed., Grand Rapids, Mich.: Zondervan Publishing House, 1976), p. 240.

10. See 2 Corinthians 12:7, NIV.

11. See 1 Corinthians 10:13, James 4:6-8, and 1 Peter 5:8-10.

12. Smith, p. 146.

13. See Psalm 37:1-8.

Chapter 5: The Bigger Picture

1. See Ruth 4:13-16 and 2:12.

2. See Proverbs 3:17.

3. Oswald Chambers, *My Utmost for His Highest* (New York: Dodd, Mead & Company, 1935), p. 25.

4. Ephesians 3:20, TLB.

5. Charles Stanley, "Is God Really in Everything?" *In Touch*.

Chapter 6: Restfully Sure of God's Loving Control

1. See Philippians 4:4-7.

2. See 1 Timothy 6:15, Phillips.

3. Carmichael, p. 83.

4. See Romans 8:29.

5. J. Oswald Sanders, *A Spiritual Clinic* (Chicago: Moody Bible Institute, 1958), pp. 34-38.

Chapter 7: Does This End All Our Struggles

1. See Exodus 16:2-8, Numbers 14:26-35, 2 Corinthians 11:26-28.

2. See Psalm 41:4; 1 John 1:8-10, 2:3-6; John 15:4.

3. See Hebrews 4:15.

4. Larry Crabb, *Inside Out* (Colorado Springs, Colo.: NavPress, 1988), p. 36.

Chapter 8: Why Do I Find It Hard To Trust God?

1. See also Matthew 11:27 and John 14:6-11; 17:6.

2. J. I. Packer, *Knowing God* (Downers Grove, Ill.: InterVarsity Press, 1973) pp. 78, 79.

3. Hannah Whitall Smith, *The God of All Comfort* (Chicago: Moody Press, 1956), p. 11.

4. See 1 Timothy 3:16 and Hebrews 1:3, KJV.

5. See Habakkuk 1; Psalms 22, 88; Luke 7:19.

6. See 2 Corinthians 10:5.

7. Packer, p. 18.

8. Packer, p. 14.

Chapter 9: Does God Really Care About Me?

1. See 1 John 1:9 and Romans 5:8.

2. See Jeremiah 31:3.

3. J. Hart

4. A. W. Tozer, *The Knowledge of the Holy* (San Francisco: Harper & Row, Publishers, 1961), p. 88.

Chapter 10: Unoffended with the Unexplained

1. Alvera Mickelson, "Why Did God Let It Happen?" *Christianity Today*, 16 March 1984, p. 22.

2. See Matthew 11:2-6.

3. William Cowper, 1774

4. Elisabeth Elliot, *On Asking God Why* (Old Tappan, N.J.: Fleming H. Revell Company, 1989), p. 10.

5. See Psalm 103:13, 14.

6. Philip Yancey, *Where Is God When It Hurts?* (Grand Rapids, Mich.: Zondervan Publishing House, 1977), pp. 66, 67, 77.

7. See John 13:7 and 21:20-22.

8. Oswald Chambers, p. 198.

9. See Psalm 46:10 and Job 23:10.

10. Anna L. Waring, 1850.

Chapter 11: Am I Just a Passive Puppet?

1. See Mark 16:15; Matthew 5:14-16, 6:33; 2 Thessalonians 3:10.

2. See the book of Esther, especially noting 2:17, 21, 22; 3:8-15; 4:11-14.

3. See 2 Corinthians 10:5, Romans 12:2, Ephesians 4:22-24.

4. R. Arthur Mathews, *Born for Battle* (Robesonia, Penn.: OMF Books, 1978), p. 14.

5. See Deuteronomy 9:16-29.

6. See Deuteronomy 9:19.

7. See 2 Corinthians 12:7-10.

8. See Matthew 26:39-46.

9. See 2 Thessalonians 3:1-5; James 1:2-5, 5:14-16; 1 Peter 4:12-14.

10. Colossians 4:12. (See also Ephesians 1:15-19; Colossians 1:9-12; 2 Thessalonians 2:16, 17.)

11. Elliot, p. 17.

12. See John 14:16-18, Romans 8:9, 1 Corinthians 6:19.

13. Stephen F. Olford, "Filled to the Brim—With Him," *Moody*, July/August 1983, p. 108.

14. James H. Mc Conkey, *The Threefold Secret of the Holy Spirit* (Lincoln, Neb.: Back to the Bible Broadcast), p. 35.

Chapter 12: Attitude: Gratitude

1. NIV (italics added).

2. Michael Baughen, *Breaking the Prayer Barrier* (Wheaton, Ill.: Harold Shaw Publishers, 1981), pp. 72, 73.

3. Ephesians 5:11, NIV. (See also Ephesians 5:3-13, 2 Corinthians 6:14-18.)

4. Haddon Robinson, *Psalm Twenty-three* (Chicago: Moody Press, 1968), p. 51.

5. See Exodus 15:24; 16:2, 3, 8; 17:2, 3; Deuteronomy 1:26, 27.

6. See Joshua 4:20-24.

7. See Exodus 15:1-18; Joshua 24:1-13; 2 Samuel 22; Psalm 107; Nehemiah 9; Luke 1:46-55, 67-79; Acts 7, 13:16-41.

8. F. B. Meyer, *Christ in Isaiah* (Grand Rapids, Mich.: Zondervan Publishing House, 1950), p. 113.

9. Verna Birkey and Jeanette Turnquist, *Building Happy Memories and Family Traditions* (Old Tappan, N.J.: Fleming H. Revell Company, 1980), p. 120.

Chapter 13: The Bottom Line

1. See Hebrews 12:26-28.

2. Lawrence J. Crabb, *Basic Principles of Biblical Counseling* (Grand Rapids, Mich.: Zondervan, 1975), p. 65.

3. See John 13:34; Romans 12:9, 10, 13; Hebrews 10:24, 25.

4. Crabb, *Basic Principles of Biblical Counseling*, p. 70.

5. See Jeremiah 2:13.

6. Meyer, *Great Verses Through the Bible*, p. 390.

7. Chambers, p. 212.